COMMERCIALIZATION
OF THE OCEANS

MICHAEL H. SEDGE

COMMERCIALIZATION
OF THE OCEANS

Franklin Watts
New York / London / Toronto / Sydney / 1987
An Impact Book

Library of Congress Cataloging-in-Publication Data
Sedge, Michael H.
Commercialization of the oceans.

(A Science impact book)
Bibliography: p.
Includes index.
Summary: Discusses commercial food, mineral, and
energy resources found in the sea and explores the
possibilities and problems involved in enterprises
such as fishing, ocean mining, and ocean farming.
1. Marine resources—Juvenile literature.
[1. Marine resources] I. Title. II. Series.
GC1016.5.S43   1987   333.91′64   86-24741
ISBN 0-531-10326-9

*This book is for my wife, Gabriella,
and children, Amanda and Daniele.*

CONTENTS

Chapter One
*Commercialization
of the Ocean*
13

Chapter Two
*A History of Ocean
Commercialization*
19

Chapter Three
Marine Biotechnology
34

Chapter Four
Food from the Sea
42

Chapter Five
Ocean Farming
54

Chapter Six
A Sea of Resources
77

Chapter Seven
Energy from the Ocean
99

Chapter Eight
*The Ocean and
Commercial Waste*
108

Selected Reading
122

Index
125

My sincere thanks to all those who
assisted in making this book a reality,
especially my editor, Henry Rasof;
Rita R. Colwell; Lee Smith;
Charles A. Black; Lynn A. Greenwalk;
Blue Magruder; and John Marchi.

OTHER BOOKS BY
MICHAEL H. SEDGE

Dive Italy
The Naples Guidebook
Welcome to Naples
Welcome to the Med

COMMERCIALIZATION
OF THE OCEANS

CHAPTER ONE

COMMERCIALIZATION OF THE OCEAN

The ocean. It makes up seventy-one percent of the earth's surface, nearly 400 billion gallons (1.5 trillion liters) of water, yet is one of the rarest substances in our solar system.

For thousands of years we have drawn life from the ocean and voyaged upon it. Only in the last thirty-five years, however, have we begun to comprehend the true complexity and life-sustaining importance of the ocean. Today, many experts believe that this shifting liquid body that blankets more than seven-tenths of the earth's surface may hold the key to our future needs.

Some scientists have estimated that the earth can comfortably support 1 or 2 billion people. Our current population is already more than double the latter figure, and by the year 2100 the world population will probably be close to 11 billion. We are therefore faced with the problem of how, with ever-decreasing food, energy, mineral, and other resources, to provide for our exploding population.

The answer, according to some, is ocean commercialization, whereby businesses would be encouraged to research, develop, harvest, and market the ocean's resources for profit.

Managing the resources of the sea represents a major challenge. There are companies already meeting this challenge head-on. Others are planning to join them. Much of the progress thus far however, has been made without considering the side effects such commercialization may have. Already some experts speculate about the increased levels of pollution that may come with ocean exploitation, resulting in new health risks to humans through the consumption of contaminated seafoods and direct infection on some beaches. Certain projects may dramatically influence marine habitats; others may cause changes to coastlines. Jobs may be affected, as may various areas of international politics. And these are merely a few of the potential or already-known side effects.

Ocean commercialization has already changed the way we live. Nearly everyone comes into daily contact with a product somehow linked to the sea. Salt, soda, toothpaste, cosmetics, iodine, nonfat creams, canned meats, ice cream, thread, filters, paint emulsifiers, photographic film, fertilizers, gas and oil—all contain by-products of the ocean.

"Since seawater covers so much of earth's surface, it is natural to look to the sea for our food, our energy, and, ultimately, our minerals," writes ocean pioneer Jacques-Yves Cousteau. "The sea . . . is man's only hope. . . ."

While many agree with Cousteau's observation, there are also those opposed to making the ocean a business without first finding out what the consequences will be. One such person is Christopher Roosevelt, president of The Oceanic Society, who believes that because of our history of mismanagement of land and air resources we should approach the exploration of the oceans from a fairly cautious perspective. The responsibility of proving the harmlessness of their activities on the marine environment, according to Roosevelt, should be placed on those involved in commercial exploration.

"Let us recognize the driving force of economics and/or

politics, but let us also insist upon thorough and comprehensive scientific data and assessment. Then, and only then, can we be comfortable that our advanced and advancing society has dealt intelligently with the health of the oceans."

FARMING THE OCEAN

Aquaculture—farming of the ocean to produce new supplies of fish and plants, rather than simply harvest what nature provides—is a good example of an enterprise with great potential that also has various drawbacks. Aquaculture currently accounts for approximately 10 million tons of the total world fish production of 80 million tons per year. But there are problems related to such ocean farming.

Saltwater aquaculture is still expensive, making it an unfeasible solution at this time to the global food problem. Reared fish are subject to infections that, if not controlled, destroy or greatly damage harvests. Unexpected changes in the condition of coastal waters where aquaculture is conducted can also be disastrous for the ocean farmer.

Another drawback of ocean farming is that these enterprises come into conflict with small-scale traditional fishing operations, many of whom face difficulties because they are unable to compete with growing commercial enterprises.

In an attempt to overcome such problems a number of commercial enterprises in Japan, Canada, the Soviet Union, and the United States have gone into "sea ranching" with fish such as the Pacific salmon. These operations rear young fish that are released into the ocean for later harvest as they come upriver to spawn. The result is greater takes of adult fish and increased profits. At times, sea ranchers are hindered by nonparticipating fishing fleets that catch the adult salmon in open water. This decreases the river harvest of the sea ranchers and cuts into their profits, despite the fact that they alone have made an investment in rearing the young fish.

ENERGY

The sea is also a source of energy for humanity. The tidal shift of water can be used to turn turbines and produce electricity. This new method of producing energy has already been employed by the Soviets, the French, and the Chinese. A tidal hydroelectric dam energy system currently projected for eastern Canada will produce an estimated 4,560 megawatts of power, more than three times the output of the Hoover Dam on the Colorado River in the United States. Tidal projects generate no pollution; nor do they stimulate the controversy surrounding nuclear energy projects.

There are, however, some problems associated with the use of such energy systems. Fish living in the tide waters may be killed as they are forced through the turbines, damaging such areas for sport as well as for commercial fishing. Such projects may also cause coastal flooding and destroy wildlife feeding grounds.

The sea is also an important source of oil and natural gas. Twenty-two percent of the world's oil is presently obtained from offshore oil wells. However, these recovery methods are not without controversy. Oil spills ruin beaches and kill wildlife, oil rigs spoil views, and protests have been heard in the United States about the way the government leases oil rights to oil companies.

MINERAL RESOURCES

An area now being studied for its commercial potential is ocean mineral mining. The United States once possessed rich mineral resources. It is not that way anymore. Ninety percent of our bauxite for aluminum and 100 percent of the chromite used to make stainless steel is imported. Even 80 percent of the nickel used to purchase bubble gum in supermarket machines comes from outside our country.

Geologists have discovered large deposits of manganese,

nickel, copper, and cobalt, as well as traces of molybdenum, titanium, vanadium, and other metals in much of the world's oceans. These deep-sea minerals, which have important uses in industry, are most frequently found in lump forms known as nodules. Nodules are sometimes found in extremely great concentrations.

Though deep-sea mining is an awesome task, the U.S. Bureau of Mines estimates that by 1990 the ocean mining industry may be providing the world with a substantial part of its important minerals.

Harvesting the ocean's rare and valuable minerals could be a positive venture for many nations. At the same time, the probing of deep-seabed minerals is certain to have profound effects on international politics, trade, and national-defense issues. Many of these metals, for example, are essential for the production of weapons and military airplanes (and are often called "strategic" metals).

COMMERCIAL WASTE

A very controversial topic of ocean exploitation is that of commercial dumping and incineration. For centuries human societies have used the ocean as a dump. As the population has grown and industrialization occurred, such dumping has increased. Toxic and radioactive materials have been deposited in the open sea, along with an increasing flow of sewage. As a consequence, the marine environment has suffered.

Even with the increased environmental awareness of the last fifteen or so years, the pollution has not gone away. In fact, it has increased. There is now a need for scientists and engineers to combine technologies to combat the side effects of ocean commercialization. Each area of exploitation is complex, costing billions of dollars in research, technology, and labor. Each realm of commercialization has unique problems that must be overcome.

The oceans have great potential for feeding humankind, providing energy and mineral wealth, and perhaps for doing more. Right now some programs and industries are going strong. Others are in the planning stages. Still others are too complicated to begin. Some are merely pipe dreams. If we are going to utilize the resources of the ocean, we will have to do so carefully.

CHAPTER TWO

A HISTORY OF OCEAN COMMERCIALIZATION

More than 200,000 years ago, Paleolithic societies enjoyed the benefits of ocean resources. Archaeological finds have revealed that these primitive peoples maintained diets of seafood, using crude bone harpoons to capture fish in shallow waters and collecting mussels, clams, oysters, lobsters, and crabs. The Neolithic peoples, who lived between 10,000 and 5,000 B.C., refined the fishing techniques of their predecessors and used bone-carved hooks, nets, even boats.

Other archaeological finds record that the invention of boats also enabled early peoples to travel and explore the oceans and their tributaries. Egyptian stone carvings tell of a voyage by Queen Hatshepsut in about 1500 B.C. The Minoans of Crete were noted seafarers, exploring much of the Mediterranean Sea. The Greeks too were great sailors, though their explorations and waterway trading were short-lived due to a powerful Phoenician fleet. The Phoenicians, the first real seafarers, sailed from Tyre and Sidon to ports in Spain, Greece, Italy, and North Africa.

By the fourth century B.C., Mediterranean trade routes were well established. In 325 B.C., early European sea travelers in search of tin made their way into the Atlantic, greatly expanding ocean commerce.

China was also involved in early ocean exploration. Under the Chou, Ch'in, and Han dynasties (1000 B.C.– 100 A.D.), boats were constructed in China for fishing, international trade, and defense. Early Chinese technology brought new designs to seagoing vessels and added such innovations as the sternpost rudder, which the Europeans quickly adapted. By the end of the first century A.D., Chinese fleets had established trade routes not only along their own coasts but also throughout the Indian Ocean and, by way of the Red Sea, into the Roman Empire.

COMMERCIAL FISHING
DEVELOPMENTS

At the same time that humans were discovering that the sea facilitated transportation and trade, they were finding that the sea's food resources were so plentiful that an industry could be established based on seafood.

In 1250 B.C., dried fish was a popular commercial trade product in the Persian Gulf. The ancient Greeks devised fish traps, while the Phoenicians established commercial fishing villages throughout the Mediterranean Sea.

From 400 B.C. until the fifth century A.D., port towns of the Roman Empire profited by catering to the Romans' taste for tuna, swordfish, sturgeon, mackerel, eel, oysters, and sea urchins. Fishing became so popular, in fact, that seafood and other ocean products were frequently used as subjects for wall paintings; such paintings were found among the ruins of ancient Pompeii.

During the Middle ages (A.D. 500–1500) the North Sea's rich fish population caused an expansion of commercial fishing in Europe. Through this period the herring was praised for its high trade value in poems and songs. By the late thirteenth century fishing ports such as Hull, Grimsby, and Barking had been established along the coast of Eng-

Sea fauna played a major role in the lives of the people of ancient civilizations. This is a wall painting from a home in Pompeii, Italy.

land. It was also during this era that North German merchants established the Hanseatic League to exploit the sea, including its fisheries.

As time passed and boats became larger and stronger, fishing fleets ventured farther from their home ports. Fishing with hook and line, Portuguese fishermen began to fish schools of cod off the Newfoundland and North American coasts. To keep their catches from spoiling, they preserved them with salt. Slowly fishermen from other nations began to leave the shallow bays and offshore fishing grounds and head for open waters.

By the late 1500s, more than a thousand commercial fishing vessels from various countries were operating in American waters. Most worked along the Grand Banks, where cold Labrador currents meet the Gulf Stream. The confluence of these currents stirs up chemical nutrients that fertilize minute drifting plants called phytoplankton, which many small fish feed upon. The natural richness of this zone made possible large catches of herring, cod, and haddock.

Sail trawlers, sailboats rigged with trawling nets, opened a new era in commercial fishing in the 1820s. Although clumsy, the new fishing technique provided greater catches than ever before, and within twenty years the rich banks of the North Sea had been dramatically exploited.

A great surge took place in the fishing industry in 1840 when sails were replaced by steam engines. Suddenly one could fish without relying on the wind. By 1890 trawlers were venturing to Iceland and many other parts of the world.

The next major development in commercial fishing came about in 1893, when early sail trawling nets were replaced by the otter trawls. This new system gave fishermen more control over the net's movement and, as a result, increased catches.

In spite of more modern methods of catching fish and shellfish, diving for seafood is still popular.

The introduction of gasoline engines in 1910 and diesel engines in 1921 enabled further expansion. Now, no waters were beyond reach.

MARINE MAMMAL BUSINESS

During the mid-1500s it was learned that whale by-products could be sold for the commercial production of oil, soaps, cooking fats, and varnishes. Soon, specially designed whaling boats began to sail the oceans in search of these large marine mammals.

Dominated by American whalers, the industry grew rapidly in the eighteenth and nineteenth centuries. By 1850, catches of blue and fin whales soared as harpoons with explosive heads were introduced. This marked the beginning of a golden age for whaling. This new system for killing whales was so effective that by 1925 the whaling industry had incorporated large, oceangoing factory ships for on-the-spot processing.

Over the next fifty years, sonar, radar, and search aircraft were utilized to hunt whales, making the whales easy prey.

The fat and protein of whales could be used to make many products. This led to a large demand for whales. As a result, the whaling industry was soon killing these animals without regard for the future. Eventually, the larger species, like the blue whale, were hunted to near extinction.

Another marine mammal, the Alaskan fur seal, had been hunted for centuries by the people of Greenland. The Greenlanders used the animal's fat to fuel oil lamps and fires, the meat for food, the skin for clothing and tents, the bladder for harpoon floats, the bones for tools and sewing needles, and the blood as a soup base.

During the late 1600s, hunters began killing these mammals for the commercial value of their fur. More intensive exploitation of the Alaskan fur seal began in 1786

An old print showing a whaling scene.

*Whales tied to the stern of a ship. Scenes like
this will eventually disappear as the whale population
dwindles and more and more countries ban whaling.*

when they were discovered beaching on the Bering Sea's Pribilof Islands. Here millions of fur seals gathered for breeding each year, easy prey for the commercial hunter. As demand for fur-seal coats grew in the civilized world, kills by American and Russian sealers increased until in 1910 only 200,000 animals remained. International restrictions were put into effect in 1911 limiting annual kills to 50,000. Today, these creatures number roughly 4 million.

JEWELRY

Artisans of the past also found profit in the ocean's resources. Cameo jewelry carved from colorful conch shells has been found among the archaeological remains of Sumerian cultures of Mesopotamia and the Minoan civilization on Crete. These date back to about 4000 B.C. Ancient cameos have also been discovered in tombs of Egyptian aristocrats as well as in parts of China, where they often decorated the shields of warriors. Cameos were introduced

Seashells make attractive jewelry.

into Greece during the Hellenistic period and filtered into the Roman culture by the first century A.D.

Despite its ups and downs in popularity over the centuries, cameo art remains a profitable commerce even today, with certain nations of the West Indies, Africa, and the Bahamas collecting and selling red or rosaniline shells to cameo factories in southern Italy and China.

Another jewel of the sea that has followed the course of history is the pearl. Long before 3500 B.C., Near East and Asian societies realized the commercial value of these saltwater gems. For them, pearls were a supreme treasure, an outward sign of one's wealth.

Egyptian queens prized pearls, as did the Greeks and Romans. Pearl earrings, necklaces, and pins were designed and crafted for the ruling families or anyone else who could afford to wear them. From the Renaissance until the mid-twentieth century, divers gathered pearl-producing oysters from the Indian Ocean, the Pacific, and the waters of the New World. Until the end of World War II, most of the world's pearl supply came from the Persian Gulf and the tiny island of Bahrain, where pearl industries employed thousands of divers.

With the economy of Persian Gulf countries shifting to one based on oil, the commerce of pearls has moved into artificial cultivation. China, the world's leading cultivator, produces 50 to 80 tons of pearls each year, selling them to foreign markets such as the United States and Japan, where they are used in the production of medicines, cosmetics, toothpaste, and, naturally, jewelry.

When used for purposes other than jewelry, pearls are normally ground into a powder. This powder contains calcium carbonate, a substance that can be made into pills that are beneficial to pregnant women and to people who suffer from fatigue, tooth decay, excess stomach acid, and allergies. When added to toothpaste, this powder acts as a tooth whitener and fortifier.

MARINE PRODUCTS FOR
HUMAN NEEDS

Long before scientists discovered the anticoagulant and antibiotic properties of certain algae (probably known to you as seaweed) or other aquatic plants, the Chinese and Japanese were utilizing them for their healing properties. As far back as 3000 B.C. they had discovered that various types of algae could be used in the treatment of goiter and glandular troubles. As time passed, Far Eastern and eventually European cultures used seaweeds to reduce fevers and prevent scurvy (a vitamin C deficiency once common throughout the world), and as laxatives and vermifuges (agents that rid the body of parasites).

Since the sixteenth century, Japan's Tokyo Bay has been one of the world's largest sites of algae cultivation. Algae (singular: alga) produced here, including the red alga Porphyra, is used not only for medicinal purposes but in soaps, sauces, macaroni, and a variety of other products. Algae processing is a large industry in Japan, employing more than half a million workers. Hawaii, too, has found a food source in aquatic vegetation. During the past century, seventy-five different types of seaweed have been adapted to the cuisine of these tropical islands.

Fish farming, like seaweed harvesting, has been practiced for a long time. To enhance their diet, the Chinese, in 1100 B.C., established one of the world's first aquaculture practices. The Chinese have continued such farming right up to the present.

With the exception of a few small oyster beds established by the Roman Emperor Nero in the first century A.D., fish farming was not practiced in Europe until the Middle Ages.

Despite their lack of involvement in aquaculture, early Europeans were extremely interested in marine species that might prove useful; sponges were among the first ocean products adapted for human use. Greek sponge divers, in

These fishermen are cleaning and trimming sponges in Florida, where harvesting sponges is a significant industry.

fact, are often the subject of ornamental paintings found on vases and other household utensils. By the sixth century B.C., sponge commerce was well established, including harvesting sponges from the ocean floor, drying, cleaning, and selling them for use in homes and public baths.

NEW AREAS OF COMMERCIALIZATION

Though the sea had been an area of both commercial and scientific interest for centuries, it was not until December 30, 1872, when the British ship HMS *Challenger* made a 3½-year, round-the-world cruise to gather scientific data relating to the oceans, that modern oceanography—the study of the ocean environment—was established as a scientific field.

As part of the *Challenger's* world expedition, the ship dredged fist-sized masses called nodules from several sites on the seafloor, but most notably on the Agulhas Bank, which extends from the southern tip of Africa. The nodules contained manganese, copper, zinc, and other minerals; phosphorite, which could be used for phosphate fertilizer; red clay, containing aluminum and copper; globigerina ooze, a source of cement lime; diatomaceous ooze, which could be used for silica; and barium spherules (a spherule is a small sphere). Each of these had commercial potential. The fact that they now could be mined collectively made the possibilities that much greater. The rich resources of the *Challenger's* nodule collection, however, would not be realized for another eighty-three years, when the systematic study of mineral distribution began.

Though the extraction of sea minerals probably dates to prehistoric times, the first written account comes from China, where in 2200 B.C. sodium chloride, or common salt, was obtained by solar evaporation of seawater. The Egyptians, Greeks, and Romans also utilized this process to reap ocean salt. Despite this early beginning, not until the late seventeenth century did taking salt from the ocean become a profit-making commerce along the Atlantic coasts, and not until the mid-nineteenth century in the Pacific.

Crude soda and potash were first extracted by the Scottish peoples in 1720. Shortly thereafter they learned the process for obtaining iodine from seaweed.

From 1872 to 1876 the HMS *Challenger* made its famed expedition under the direction of Sir C. Wyville Thomson. More than twelve thousand geological samples were collected during the extensive voyage, including the now famous manganese nodules.

In 1923, solar evaporation was used for the first time in San Francisco to produce magnesium chloride and gypsum from seawater. By 1931, small but profitable businesses had been developed in many parts of the world to market these minerals, as well as bromine and potassium chloride.

Soda, which comes from sodium, is commonly used in cooking. Potash comes from potassium and is widely used as a fertilizer. Magnesium chloride is an important substance for the chemical industry. Gypsum is used to enrich soil and, just as important, as a component in the production of plaster of paris and plasterboard. Bromine has a wide range of uses, including as an ingredient in pharmaceuticals and photographic materials, and as a component of high-octane gasoline. Potassium chloride, like potash, is processed for fertilizer, though it is also utilized in other chemical substances.

It was not until after the scientific study of the HMS *Challenger*'s deep-sea nodules in 1958, however, that large international industries with technical engineering capabilities began to display an interest in mining the ocean floor.

While deep-sea mineral mining was developing, offshore oil wells were being drilled from piers along the southern coast of California. The year was 1891. Twenty-eight years later, a dramatic push would be given to drilling movement with the development of the Elwood Field near Santa

Barbara. Once established, offshore drilling became the fastest developed and most profitable of all marine resource-recovery efforts.

By 1970, the U.S. Geological Survey estimated that more than fifty companies were operating more than seven thousand wells in the Gulf of Mexico. Other productive areas of offshore oil and natural gas included the Persian Gulf, the North Sea, the South China Sea, the Caspian Sea, the Arctic's Beaufort Sea, and the coasts of California, Alaska, and Lake Maracaibo. Today, offshore drilling provides an estimated 12.5 million barrels per day, some 22 percent of the world's oil and much of its natural gas. (One barrel of petroleum equals 42 gallons, or 159 liters.)

Quite clearly, the ocean has played a role in the history and development of societies the world over.

CHAPTER THREE

MARINE
BIOTECHNOLOGY

Marine biotechnology is one of the most exciting areas of contemporary ocean research. But exactly what is biotechnology? How is it applied to the marine world? And what role does it play in ocean commerce?

Biotechnology is the manipulation of the genetic material of living organisms. Using this process, genetic engineers—who are actually biologists and chemists rather than engineers—are able to design or alter the genetic material of marine animals and plants to enable them to do things they cannot do naturally, much as traditional engineers can design a machine to perform a specific function.

Biotechnology had its beginnings in 1970, when scientists discovered how to remove deoxyribonucleic acid, or DNA—a complex chemical found in all living things that controls their size, shape, and functions—from one living organism and place it into another. This was an important biological discovery, particularly useful in the field of medicine.

Genetic engineers also are able to reproduce some genetic material as well as other substances in artificial environments. Some of these substances are produced in large quantities and sold for industrial use.

While biotechnology makes use of several different discoveries in biology, one of the most important is the ability to reproduce antibodies, which are an important part of our immune system, outside the human body. Once this system was perfected, researchers began looking for new sources of antibodies. One place they looked was the ocean. In fact, the sea is turning out to be a gigantic medicine chest.

For instance, sponges were found to be a source of antibiotics. In one instance, chemicals from a species of sponge killed a harmful bacteria resistant to penicillin. The electric eel, it was learned, contains a large amount of a substance essential to proper human nerve function. A chemical in the stonefish is found to decrease high blood pressure in animals.

Sea fans, a type of coral, have been found to be a source of antibiotics and the group of medicines known as steroids.

While examining extracts of Pacific anemones, scientists discovered that one of the extracts contained a chemical substance with potential for treating heart disease. This substance could have more value than some medicines now being used, such as digitalis, which produce bad side effects in heart patients.

Each of these natural marine substances can be artificially reproduced for the benefit of humanity and advancement of medicine in general through biotechnological means.

Though there have been many discoveries, we have as yet only peeked into the medicine chest. Numerous marine species have yet to be studied for their medical secrets.

While many nations have charged ahead in the application of biotechnology, particularly in medicine, others are lagging behind because of a lack of microbiologists, poor backgrounds in the area of antibiotics, insufficient training of genetic engineers, and poor links between research and industry. Another problem that many nations face is generating financial support for research and development. To overcome this hurdle, however, some countries are uniting forces under cooperative projects.

INDUSTRIAL CHEMICALS

Headway is also being made in the research and development of species that can be used in the production of industrial chemicals. In fact, many of the two hundred biotechnology companies in the United States market specialty chemicals such as carrageenin, which is used to extend the freshness of foods and related products, from evaporated milk to toothpaste. Other chemicals derived through marine sources include unusual sugars, polysaccharides, and enzymes, which are used in detergents and other products that act to break down molecules. Algal lipids, used as a base for various waxes and fat products, have also been taken from the sea.

As research continues, many new chemicals are being discovered. A new form of polyether, for example, has been isolated from a black sponge commonly found along the Pacific coast of Japan and a Caribbean sponge found in the Florida Keys.

Many chemicals are derived from plants such as red seaweed and agarose. Biotechnological methods of modifying such plants are being employed in a limited fashion at present. Researchers screen various species in search of desirable traits such as fast growth. Once such a trait is located in a particular plant, biologists and chemists can isolate the gene that causes the plant's fast growth and transfer that gene to other plants. If they are successful, the other plants will then have a faster growth rate.

This method has been used to create a number of hybrid species. The reproduction and growth of marine species used for the production of special industrial chemicals can be manipulated in artificial cultures.

AQUACULTURE

Two of the major drawbacks of aquaculture are slow growth rates and disease. Producing species that have a natural resistance to common culture diseases as well as fast growth rates could increase harvests and, at the same time, decrease costs. Biotechnology applications can help control the growth and general health of certain marine species, promising potential benefits for the aquaculture industry.

For more than a decade, research in these areas has been carried out on marine shrimp, crayfish, blue crab, salmon and other finfish, and on shellfish such as oysters and clams.

At the University of California at Santa Barbara, Professor D.E. Morse has developed a simple and inexpensive method to increase the frequency of reproduction of abalone by adding hydrogen peroxide to seawater in which the abalone live. Considering that abalone sold for twenty to thirty dollars a pound in 1985, this biological discovery could result in increased profits for those involved in the artificial rearing of abalone.

Biological experiments, including the introduction of various natural substances into marine animals such as crayfish, have increased some species' resistance to infections. Also, through genetic engineering, certain shellfish and finfish have overcome various diseases.

The causes of many diseases contributing to the loss of aquaculture stocks are still not yet known, nor do we have ways to control the spreading of all the diseases whose causes are known. Because of the many species of shellfish and finfish available in cultures, however, researchers have excellent opportunities for experimentation with gene manipulation. With time, it is believed that biotechnology will enhance the productivity of aquacultures from the early stages, at present a high-risk part of the life cycle, to the harvest.

BIODEGRADING

Natural biodegrading is an area of marine biotechnology that holds vast commercial potential. Biodegrading is the decomposition, or dissolving, of wastes. Unlike natural products, many artificial compounds are relatively resistant to decomposition. These create special problems for waste treatment and the environment.

It has been discovered that many man-made compounds can be dissolved using certain substances that come from various marine sources. A scientific report on marine biotechnology and its industrial potential that appeared in the spring 1984 issue of *Oceanus* magazine indicated that this method of biodegrading is already commonly practiced for removing nitrogen, a potential pollutant, from wastewater.

In Japan, biologists and chemists have successfully used genetic engineering to cultivate large quantities of a bacteria and algae mixture used for treating some industrial wastes.

Because of industry's limited and somewhat cautious interest in biodegradation, progress in this area is slow. The fact that biological waste treatments have proven successful in many areas might justify the mass-scale production and marketing of biodegradation substances through various methods of genetic engineering. Some feel that this will come about in the near future.

FOULING

A costly burden for any operation carried out in the ocean environment is "fouling," the attachment of organisms such as barnacles to the surfaces of submerged objects. Biotechnology is currently being applied to this problem in hopes of discovering a method of control that will be effective yet not damage marine species.

At Duke University's Marine Laboratory in Beaufort, North Carolina, researchers are exploring the use of two natural repellents extracted from whip coral as possible

Barnacles like these grow on the hulls of ships.

fouling deterrents. One of the substances acts to temporarily paralyze larvae while the other discourages the permanent settlement of the mature organism upon surfaces.

According to Dan Rittschof, a Duke research associate, neither substance damages the fouling organism; it just keeps it from evolving into the adult form. Though such research is promising, scientists are still faced with the problem of introducing such antifouling substances into forms for commercial use. One possibility being studied is to introduce the natural repellent substances into aquatic plants that could be grown around docks, platforms, and other areas where fouling is a major problem.

At the same time that they are looking for ways to control fouling, scientists are discovering uses for fouling organisms. For example, the natural cement of barnacles has been found to remain effective in the face of high pressure, temperatures up to 400 degrees Fahrenheit (200°C), strong acids, solvents, and bacteria. If a glue with these properties could be successfully manufactured, many businesses, especially the medical industry, might find it advantageous.

THE BIOTECHNOLOGY BUSINESS

Inasmuch as the application of biotechnology holds extraordinary promise for the marine sciences, lack of coordination and follow-through among universities, research organizations, and the public and private sectors often slow down progress. Many potential beneficiaries, in addition, are unwilling to invest in long-term projects that do not insure a profitable return.

Some early investors have made fortunes with small biotechnology companies even though many others have yet to make a profit. Some of the original researchers, too, have made fortunes by joining new companies or by establishing companies of their own.

Old-line pharmaceutical and chemical companies such as Du Pont, Eli Lilly, and Schering-Plough have also entered the field. As a result, some of the smaller, younger companies have faced bankruptcies or cutbacks, despite the likely long-term profitability of biotechnology.

It is estimated that in the United States only five thousand people are employed in biotechnology research and development. Depending on how we define the field, this number could be somewhat higher but not by much. Five thousand people are not very many when you consider that in the United States more than 100 million people are employed in all fields. In fact, it is less than one worker in twenty thousand. One reason for this is that most of the basic research that made the commercialization of biotechnology possible was, and continues to be, done in universities.

In terms of economic and employment advantages, biotechnology appears to be restricted to a very select group. In terms of social benefits, though, this field offers much. We are already enjoying a better style of life because of discoveries through marine biotechnology. But research has merely begun; thousands of sea animals, plants, and minute organisms remain to be studied for their potential benefits to humankind.

CHAPTER FOUR

FOOD FROM
THE SEA

It was once believed that the ocean's food resources were inexhaustible. Such a belief is no longer held. Although ocean foods play an important role in the world economy and human diet, many experts feel that the pressures of population and poverty may exhaust vulnerable fishery stocks before effective controls can be devised and implemented.

Past experience has taught us that it is possible to ruin fisheries through overexploitation—sometimes in combination with climate changes or other natural forces. There is some hope of extending resources through the use of unconventional species, including various small fish, squid, and krill—small, shrimplike crustaceans. All fish resources —and their habitats—need careful research and wise management, however, if we are to continue to benefit from them.

Fish are the main source of protein—a vital body builder—for many people of the world, notably the Japanese. The average American consumes only about one-seventh the amount of fish consumed by the average Japanese. Fish are an economical way to obtain one's supply

A fisherman hauling in fish from his small boat—a scene many people picture when they think of fishing.

of protein. It comes as a surprise to most of us to learn that the amount of protein in an average serving of fish is equal to, and often higher than, that in an average serving of beef. Fish and shellfish also supply us with five times the magnesium of beef and more phosphorus than is in milk. Seafoods have from fifty to two hundred times the iodine (needed to keep our thyroid glands functioning properly) as that found in most other foods.

Fish are also used as feed for many animals. About half the fish caught in the United States, for instance, are utilized in feed for poultry, cattle, fur animals, dogs, and cats.

Seafood contributes to the world economy. According to the Food and Agriculture Organization's latest report, international trade of fishery products exceeded $32 billion. Canada's commercial fisheries led the export market that year with sales of $1.2 billion. The United States ranked second with nearly $1 billion, followed by Norway and Denmark.

When we speak of food that comes from the sea, most of us probably think of fish and shellfish, such as cod, herring, halibut, tuna, oysters, crabs, scallops, lobster, and clams. Even though a wide variety of marine life is used as food, including plants, large-scale commercial fishing is concentrated on relatively few species. The finfish is the mainstay of commercial fishing, accounting for roughly 90 percent of annual harvests. For this reason, these species must be protected. If not, the world's food supply and the lives of many people will be jeopardized.

According to the World Bank, 12 million people throughout the world support themselves by fishing. This figure does not include millions of others employed in the transportation, processing, and marketing of ocean catches. Should our ocean food resources one day become exhausted, these workers would be dramatically affected. Despite this, some experts feel the commercial fishing industry is contributing to the problem, rather than helping to solve it.

World Fishing Leaders

Country	Annual Catch in Tons
Japan	12,375,000
USSR	10,732,476
China	5,734,581
USA	4,556,800
Chile	4,375,885
Norway	3,104,543
India	2,772,000
Republic of Korea	2,640,425
Thailand	2,475,000
Indonesia	2,323,453

Normal annual catches of fish, crustaceans, molluscs, etc.
Source: FAO's "Yearbook of Fishery
Statistics of Catches and Landings," 1983, Vol. 56.

INFLUENCES IN
COMMERCIAL FISHING

Since 1940, commercial fish catches have increased nearly 250 percent as a result of improvements in the fishing industry's technology. Where once commercial fishers caught species such as yellowfin tuna one at a time, highly efficient nets are now employed in mass harvests.

To realize even greater yields, the commercial fishing industry is utilizing highly sophisticated instruments. They have become harvesters, rather than the hunters they used to be. Some ships are even rigged with experimental acoustic locating devices to find fish.

Seafood tends to spoil more rapidly than do animal protein foods like meat and eggs. Thus, to a certain extent, the fishing industry's development has been determined by the success of the techniques employed to preserve and store ocean food products.

Methods used to retard or prevent spoilage include curing by drying, smoking, salting, and use of sugar, spices, herbs, and acids such as vinegar. If decomposition is controlled, even fermentation can be used to extend the freshness of ocean harvests. Cooling with ice slows down the multiplication of microorganisms and freezing stops their multiplication altogether. Canning results in total destruction of microorganisms through a process involving extreme heat.

Drying and smoking as methods of preservation originated in prehistoric times. Salting and pickling were developed in the early dawn of the historic period. Natural ice has been used for many centuries for refrigeration. But modern, commercial-scale freezing of fish did not begin until 1844. Before long, improved icing and freezing techniques made possible the large-scale expansion of the North Atlantic fishing industries and the rapid growth of the shrimp and tuna fisheries.

After freezing, canning, greatly developed over the past century, is the most important method of food preservation used by the fishing industry; seafoods were among the first products canned. Salmon was first canned in Aberdeen, Scotland, in 1824, and it is claimed that the first salmon canned on the North American continent was packed at St. Johns, New Brunswick, in 1839, and in Maine not long after. Canning first became important on the Columbia River and developed fully when it spread to British Columbia, Alaska, northern Japan, and Siberia. Though its first cannery was not built until 1978, Alaska is the most important salmon canning center today.

As a result of modern canning and freezing techniques,

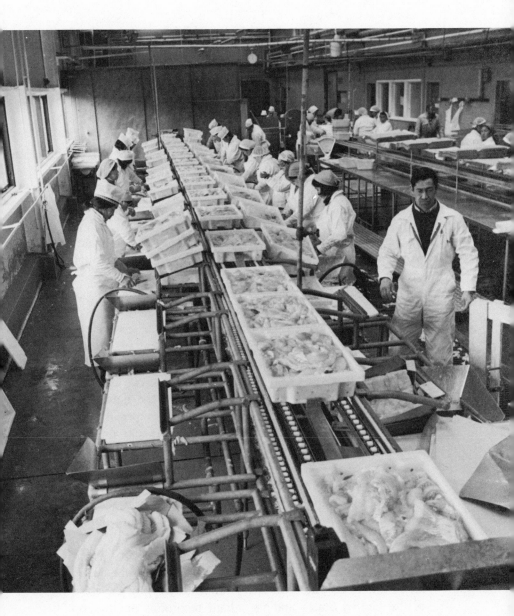

Fish processing in Greenland, where fishery resources provide the basis of the economy.

seafoods can now be enjoyed by people living thousands of miles from the sea.

Inasmuch as processing has aided the fishing industry, about 6 million tons of fish are still lost each year as a result of spoilage and waste. In addition, certain types of commercial boats discard large amounts of fish that they themselves are not interested in. The discarding of this so-called "by-catch" involves the loss of an estimated 5 million tons or more of fish per year that the people of the world need.

FISHING GROUNDS

The United Nations 1982 Law of the Sea Treaty obligated participating nations to (1) protect their fisheries through proper conservation, management, and specified enforcement measures; (2) ensure that their fisheries were not endangered by over-exploitation; (3) cooperate directly or through international fisheries organizations to ensure the conservation and optimum utilization of migratory species; (4) cooperate in order to conserve, manage, and study marine mammals; (5) adopt measures to protect and preserve rare or fragile ecosystems as well as the habitat of depleted, threatened, or endangered marine species; and (6) prevent the introduction of alien or new species into the marine environment and recognize ecologically vulnerable areas such as the Arctic. If carried out, each of these steps could be beneficial to the ocean's food resources.

The Law of the Sea Treaty also prompted nations that had not already done so to establish the right to resources along their borders.

Though the United States did not sign this treaty, President Reagan proclaimed on March 10, 1983 that the ocean area from a line 3 nautical miles (almost 6 km) off the coast of the United States and its inland territories out to 200 nautical miles (370 km) was the Exclusive Economic Zone (EEZ) of the United States. (A nautical mile is almost 800 feet longer than a "terrestrial" mile.)

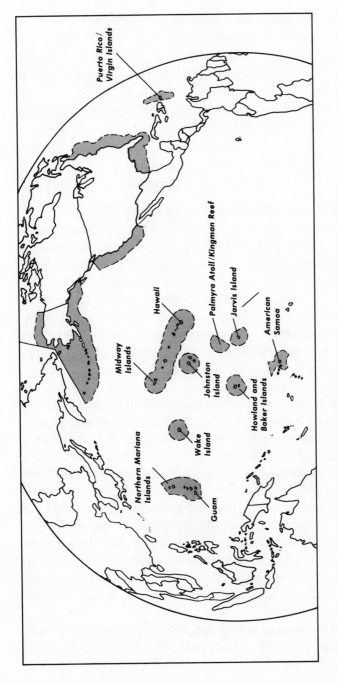

Puerto Rico/
Virgin Islands

Palmyra Atoll/Kingman Reef

Hawaii

Jarvis Island

American
Samoa

Midway
Islands

Johnston
Island

Howland and
Baker Islands

Northern Mariana
Islands

Wake
Island

Guam

The shaded areas show the Exclusive Economic
Zone claimed by the United States.

This act gave the United States jurisdiction over 3 million square nautical miles (10 million square kilometers) of commercial fishing waters, including parts of the Atlantic, Pacific, and Arctic Oceans, the Gulf of Mexico, and the Caribbean and Bering Seas. In terms of edible fish, the United States has claimed exclusive rights to an estimated 15 to 25 percent of the world total.

THE OCEAN'S DWINDLING FOOD SOURCES

Because of improved fishing methods and equipment, annual world fish catches have climbed from 22 million tons in 1948 to a level of 80 million tons. This dramatic increase has caused concern among experts regarding the possible over-exploiting of the ocean's fish stocks. Many feel, in fact, that we have already reached or exceeded the catch limits of traditional species. A good example of this is the anchoveta, which had a peak harvest in 1970 of 13 million tons. Two years later, as a result of natural events and overfishing, its population was so depleted that the annual catch of this fish was less than 2 million tons.

One possible solution to this problem is the utilization of unconventional species such as squid, krill, oysters, clams, octopus, cuttlefish, and lantern and light fish, to offset a lesser take of conventional fish species. Despite their often gruesome appearance, some deep-water species have been proven palatable. Fish living at depths of 2,600 to 3,600 feet (790 to 1,100 m) like the grenadier and red director are already being harvested in some parts of the world.

Other nontypical marine species are also being caught as food sources. Harvests of crustaceans, winkles, conch, abalones, scallops, pectens, cockles, arkshells, turtles, sea-squirts and sea urchins are increasing as traditional fish populations decline.

One of the most unique species that has been adapted to the human diet is the sea barnacle. There are approximately

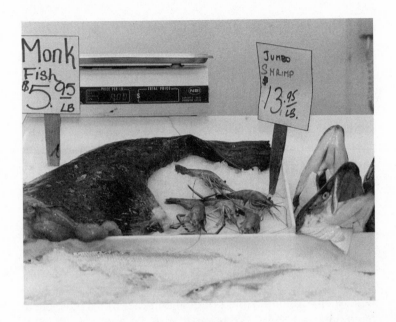

Monkfish, jumbo shrimp, and fish heads in a New York fish market. Monkfish is sometimes called "poor man's lobster," but in 1986 you could buy a whole lobster in Maine for about the same price as a pound of monkfish.

fifteen hundred known types of barnacles in the ocean, though the goose barnacle is considered the cream of the crop. In Spain, this common organism, considered a pest elsewhere, is a delicacy, bringing twenty to thirty dollars a pound (about half a kilogram) in 1985.

The obstacles of using unconventional species, however, are significant. First, most people do not take well to the taste of new foods, particularly those originating from the sea, and would have to overcome this natural aversion. New methods of packaging and preparation would be required as well as more effective fishing methods.

But there are other problems. Krill, for example, has great food-source potential. Many factors, however, inhibit extensive exploitation. There is a problem of distance, since krill stocks are primarily found in the Antarctic. There are problems of inadequate processing facilities. If these obstacles were overcome, there would still remain the problem of selling customers krill rather than traditional seafoods.

There is another problem too: A main reason for the present abundance of krill is the lack of whales that feed upon them. According to some marine biologists, mass harvesting of krill would stop the comeback of the whale.

In addition to utilizing nontraditional species, enforced laws on allowed catches could be a plus for boosting dwindling populations of ocean fish, according to the Washington-based Conservation Foundation. Currently, managers attempt to capitalize on marine-food resources to achieve optimum sustainable yields, or the greatest benefit to society that can be obtained from a fishery after biologic, socioeconomic, and political considerations have been taken into account. What must also be taken into consideration, though, are the affects, positive as well as negative, of large harvests by foreign nations.

In the past, catch limits have been established in hopes of preventing overexploitation. Because these limits were not enforced, large catches continued. A good example of this came in 1981 when the International Fisheries Commission recommended a catch of almost 200,000 tons of Baltic cod. Because nations could not agree upon this figure, the final decision was to take 272,000 tons. The ultimate catch, however, totaled nearly 380,000 tons. And the accuracy of even this figure is questionable, as underreporting of catches is often practiced.

It is obvious that a problem of international cooperation exists. It is not an easy task to place unified catch restrictions on all nations, particularly those suffering high levels of malnutrition. At the same time, is it just to establish guidelines for some nations and not others? What priorities should be used? Is it more important to protect and extend the ocean's food resources for future generations or to feed today's hungry? These are a few of the considerations that decision makers are facing. If not handled with extreme care, such problems could damage the health and economy of the entire world.

CHAPTER FIVE

OCEAN FARMING

There is no doubt that fisheries play a major role in the world economy and in helping provide adequate human nutrition. But how long can ocean fish resources be exploited before they are exhausted? The answer, according to many experts, is not much longer. Some say, in fact, that we have just about harvested many traditional food sources to the limit.

With annual harvests of nearly 80 million tons, it may be difficult to conceive of the extinction of ocean fishes. To understand that this possibility is a reality, we need only recall the nearly fatal history of the whale, the collapse of the enormous anchoveta fishery off Peru, and the disappearance of the California sardines. Already stocks of Pacific salmon, Alaska king crab, and the Atlantic's herring and striped bass have been severely depleted. In facing this problem a growing emphasis has been placed on commercial ocean farming, or aquaculture. (Technically, aquaculture is cultivation in any water; mariculture is saltwater aquaculture specifically.)

Aquaculture, the raising of marine life much as land farmers do with terrestrial plants and animals, is starting to play an important role in world fish production. This is particularly true in developing countries, where much of the world's aquaculture production occurs. Already, according to the United Nations Food and Agriculture Organization (FAO), 10 million tons of the global fish harvest is achieved through farming methods. While many developing nations are utilizing low-technology pond systems to grow various species of carp, tilapia, or mullet, other countries are applying advanced technology to greatly increase populations of finfish, shellfish, crustaceans, and even seaweed—an important ocean-farming crop.

In 1982, China, with an annual aquaculture output of slightly more than 4 million tons, was the undisputed world leader in the field. Of their 4 million tons, 800,000 tons was finfish, 1.8 million tons was shellfish, and 1.4 million tons was seaweed. Ranked second was Japan, with 249,000 tons of finfish, 285,000 tons of shellfish, and 426,000 tons of seaweed—a total of nearly a million tons. Other leaders in this growing industry include India (847,000 tons), South Korea (480,000 tons), the Soviet Union (340,000 tons), and Indonesia (199,000 tons).

The 1982 aquaculture take in the United States was 180,000 tons. While this figure falls far below that of several other countries, it is nearly twenty times greater than the U.S. aquaculture harvest of 1970. Since fish farming is greatly influenced by technology and financial support, it is estimated that the United States will soon be a world leader in aquaculture production. Already 40 percent of the oysters and nearly all of the rainbow trout, catfish, and crayfish harvested in this country are from fish farms.

THE PROTEIN ENERGY
OF FARMED FISH

One reason that aquaculture operations are growing is the greater protein value of fish over that of other food sources. In a report for the summer 1985 issue of *Science of Food*

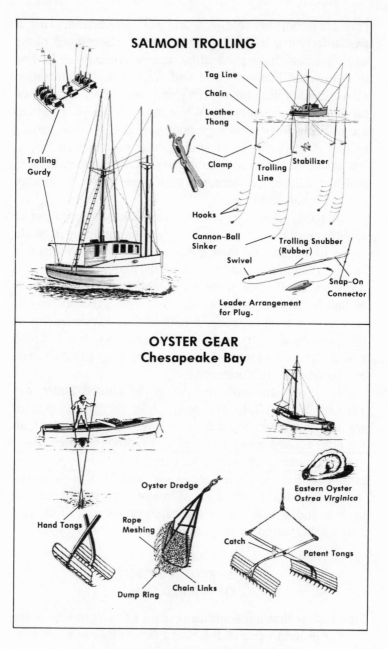

SALMON TROLLING

Tag Line

Chain

Leather Thong

Trolling Gurdy

Clamp

Trolling Line

Stabilizer

Hooks

Cannon-Ball Sinker

Trolling Snubber (Rubber)

Swivel

Snap-On Connector

Leader Arrangement for Plug.

OYSTER GEAR
Chesapeake Bay

Oyster Dredge

Eastern Oyster Ostrea Virginica

Hand Tongs

Rope Meshing

Catch

Patent Tongs

Dump Ring

Chain Links

*Four of the many traditional ways used
to catch fish and shellfish.*

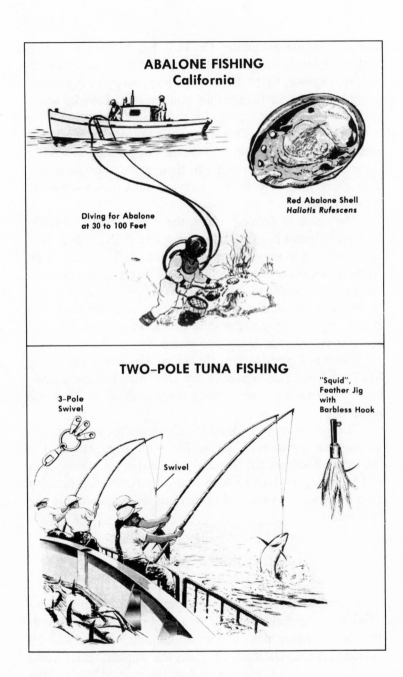

ABALONE FISHING
California

Diving for Abalone
at 30 to 100 Feet

Red Abalone Shell
Haliotis Rufescens

TWO-POLE TUNA FISHING

3-Pole
Swivel

Swivel

"Squid",
Feather Jig
with
Barbless Hook

and Agriculture magazine, Dr. R.T. Lovell, of the department of Fisheries and Allied Aquaculture at Auburn University, explains that "fish require less energy to synthesize a gram of protein than either poultry or livestock, which makes them a more energy-efficient source of protein for human consumption. This is because fish don't have to expend energy to maintain a constant body temperature like warm-blooded farm animals. In their watery surroundings, they exert relatively little energy to maintain a constant position unless they are pursuing food."

The value of farmed fish in the human diet can easily be demonstrated by comparing them with such foods as beef and pork. An average farmed fish contains 81 percent lean tissue and 5 percent fat, for a total of 112 calories per 100 grams. In comparison, beef contains 51 percent lean tissue, 34 percent fat, and a total of 323 calories for each 100 grams. Pork is 37 percent lean tissue, 42 percent fat, and has 402 calories for every 100 grams.

Whether figures such as these have influenced the eating habits of Americans is hard to say. One thing is certain, however. Americans are consuming more seafood and less red meat.

The European Economic Community is currently looking to commercial farms for such products as fish for frozen food production and substitutes for turkey rolls and hamburgers. Due to such innovations, the fish-farming crop in Europe is expected to increase by 75 percent in the near future.

ADDITIONAL ADVANTAGES TO AQUACULTURE

There are, however, reasons for commercial ocean farming other than the food value of the additional fish marketed. The ocean, being part of nature, cannot be regulated by human beings. Because of this, the supply, price, and quality of open-water harvests fluctuate considerably. Fish cultivation, like that of wheat or corn, provides a means of controlling and stabilizing much of the world fish market. As the same time, a higher quality product can be delivered to consumers through proper feeding and rapid, protected delivery of live fish to proceeding plants.

Ocean farming can be carried out in mangroves, where masses of trees grow in flooded coasts; estuaries, where tide waters connect to rivers; saltwater lagoons; shallow coastal waters; and artificial ponds linked to the sea. More than 7 million acres (11,000 square miles, or 28,000 square kilometers) of water surface are supporting aquaculture projects, according to recent estimates. Yet scientists at the Woods Hole Oceanographic Institute in Massachusetts say that the world also contains almost a billion acres (1.6 million square miles, or 4 million square kilometers) of coastal marshes adaptable to aquaculture. Developing only one-tenth of that area would result in an annual harvest of 100 million tons, more than the current total harvest of fish (by fishing *and* aquaculture).

The methods used in ocean farming are as varied as the crops themselves. Salmon, trout, catfish, marine shrimp, crayfish, crabs, sea turtles, oysters, and seaweed are all common aquaculture crops, each calling for special treatment and management.

Traditional aquaculture called for fish farmers to do little more than stock ponds. Today, aquaculture has become a science much like modern agriculture. Modern fish farmers not only use organic waste and chemical fertilizers to increase the vegetation on which their stocks feed but also employ balanced rations of direct feeding of high-protein concentrates, similar to those used with poultry and livestock.

Engineering technology, too, has assisted the aquatic entrepreneur. At the Saxbe Aqua Farm in Vancouver, British Columbia, for example, a recently installed plastic-tube feeding system automatically provides a steady, proper food diet to fish stocks while bringing down labor costs.

Such innovations have caused annual aquaculture yields, and profits, to rise steadily. For this reason, the interest of investors in aquaculture projects has also grown.

TYPES OF AQUACULTURE

Basically, aquaculture techniques fall into three categories: (1) eggs from wild parents are collected and incubated, and hatched fishes are reared to marketable sizes; (2) young fish and marine animals are captured and confined in enclosures where they mature on natural habitat foods or through supplementary feed; (3) young are reared and released into open waters to be harvested as adults.

FARMING VIA THE EGG-INCUBATION-HATCHING SYSTEM

In the first form of cultivation, operators have complete control over the life cycle of the crop. Trout, salmon, catfish, and carp are commonly farmed in this way. Much of the commercial oysters in Europe are also derived by this egg-incubation-hatching system. Aquatic farming by this method is done in stages, regardless of the individual species. In the case of the oyster, it is a ten-step process.

Producers collect adult specimens and transport them to bays or other areas protected from natural elements such as storms or waves. In the spring, when water temperatures rise, the adult oysters begin to spawn. At this point the producer lowers artificial "spat" collectors into the water on which tiny larval oysters attach themselves.

Several types of spat collectors are used today. Off the coast of France, for instance, oyster farmers merely stack semicircular tiles and lower them into the water approximately one foot from the ocean floor, so that water passes freely. On the average fifty young will gather on each tile, where they will develop into orange-colored "seed oysters."

Farming oysters in France. These people look as if they're farming vegetables, don't they?

In the winter they are pried from the tiles and transferred to growing beds or "parcs," often covered by nets to
eliminate attacks by predators. Here the oysters feed on
microscopic organisms carried by the ocean's tide. After
eighteen months the beds are dredged and the tiny shellfish
taken by barge to fattening grounds. The oysters, which
add a new layer to their shell each year, are left to grow for
about five years before they are gathered, cleansed in fresh
seawater, and commercially marketed.

CAPTURING AND REARING YOUNG

The second aquaculture technique calls for capturing young
fish and marine animals and rearing them in enclosed areas.
Because this is the simplest system of ocean farming, calling
for limited financial output in comparison to those operations requiring hatcheries, it has been adapted throughout
the world, especially for harvesting milkfish, mullet, shrimp,
oysters, and mussels.

To obtain their initial stocks, many fisheries have relied
upon the habit of pelagic fishes (those that inhabit open
seas rather than coastal waters) of gathering beneath or
near floating objects. In Indonesia, Japan, Malta, and the
Philippines, anchored rafts, logs, and bamboo mats are used
to attract and hold fish. In 1977, the Honolulu laboratory
of the Southwest Fisheries Center began a program to see
if such anchored devices would attract and hold large fishes
like tuna, and if the devices would withstand rough ocean
conditions. The devices proved to be successful in both
respects, allowing sport fishers to catch fish with minimum
bait and fishing time.

The experiment was so successful, in fact, that the State
of Hawaii implemented a statewide system of fish-
aggregating devices in 1979, initially employing twenty-
six attracting-holding devices and, in 1982, installing an
additional twenty-eight.

Though not really a farming operation, these experiments conducted off Hawaii's coast led to several new developments in open-water aquaculture. In one case, young tuna were successfully captured off the coast of Sicily, using a method similar to that of the Southwest Fisheries Center, and were reared in open-water pens.

Even though the open-water rearing environment solved common aquaculture problems dealing with water circulation, waste removal, and many cultured-fish diseases, the end results proved disastrous in this case. After several months in captivity, the natural instincts of the maturing tuna to reach the open sea caused the fish to kill themselves by ramming the webbed-metal walls of the holding pen.

Not all experiments of this type have been unsuccessful. Thousands of productive farming operations are carried out in open waters throughout the world. In Norway, entrepreneurs cultivate salmon and rainbow trout along the Atlantic coast in large floating pens. In 1981, such farming resulted in harvests of 8,000 tons, and by 1985, the take had nearly tripled.

One of the most interesting and successful stories of young aquatic animals being commercially reared is that of the Caribbean green sea turtle. In 1968, a Miami-based marine biologist, concerned with the possible extinction of the sea turtle, established the world's first turtle farm, Mariculture Ltd., on Grand Cayman Island. Mariculture Ltd. had both commercial and conservational goals.

First, an artificial beach was made where female turtles could lay eggs. In nature, less than 1 percent of all hatching turtles survive. At the farm, however, the success rate was, and is still, excellent.

Once born, turtles are transported to large tanks where they are fed and allowed to grow to adult size. At times, the farm contains as many as 78,000 turtles of various ages. Up to 60 two- to three-year-old turtles, weighing from 100 to 125 pounds (46 to 57 kg), are harvested daily. A

similar number are released into the open sea as part of the original conservation plan of Mariculture Ltd.

Cultivated turtles are 100 percent useful. From each harvested animal comes turtle meat, soup products, leather for shoes and purses, and oils used in cosmetics; from the shell comes custom jewelry items.

The Cayman government, which purchased the turtle farm in April 1983, continues to operate this multimillion-dollar aquaculture business. In addition, it has turned the unique farm into one of the island's most profitable tourist attractions.

An offshoot of the capture-and-rearing aquaculture system is polyculture. Begun by the ancient Chinese, polyculture consists of taking various species of fish and/or shellfish with different feeding habits and rearing them in the same environment.

The success of polyculture is based on the different habits of fishes coexisting in the same environment. Certain species feed on floating aquatic vegetation; others maintain diets of phytoplankton and zooplankton; still others feed primarily on the bottom. Each species finds its own "space" in the aquatic farm, growing to adulthood without encroaching on the others.

No matter what the farming technique, there is an obvious economic advantage to rearing those species that can make use of the culture system's natural foods. Supplemental feeding, however, has also proven to be financially advantageous. For instance, experiments with common carp indicated that a diet of natural aquatic vegetation yielded about 350 pounds of fish per acre (395 kilograms per hectare), while grain-fed fish yielded nearly 1,400 pounds (1,500 kilograms per hectare). Those with a protein-rich

Turtle farming on
Grand Cayman Island.

diet brought nearly 3,000 pounds (3,200 kilograms per hectare).

In addition to increased growth, most entrepreneurs also desire "crops" with fast yields. In operations where overhead costs are high, or in regions where climatic conditions affect the harvest periods, fish must reach a marketable size as rapidly as possible. One type of aquaculture that has been extremely successful in this regard is salmon ranching, which is really part of the third aquaculture type—rearing and releasing.

REARING AND RELEASING

In this method, young are reared and released into open waters to be harvested later as adults. This is possible because salmon, like certain species of ocean-going trout, are "anadromous" fish, living most of their lives in saltwater but returning to the freshwater stream of their origin to spawn. This keen homing instinct assures ranchers of a good yield some three to five years later; it makes harvesting exceedingly easy. Experience has taught, however, that there are big problems involved with this method.

The first attempt to artificially rear salmon took place in Germany around 1763. Though little was known about the salmon's unique homing instincts at that time, investigators realized that eggs could be squeezed from females, fertilized with sperm from the males, and incubated in cool flowing water until they hatched.

In the United States, researchers began studying the possibilities of salmon culturing in 1804. Sixty-six years later, along California's McCloud River, the first hatchery for Pacific salmon was built. The only function of the hatchery was to incubate eggs, without concern for the feeding or survival of the recently hatched fish, called "fry" that were immediately released into the nearby river. As a result, most of the young fish died or were consumed by predators.

A fish hatchery in Oregon.

The state of Washington developed an advanced hatchery in 1895 along the Kalama River. Here, chinook, the largest of the Pacific salmon, were not only spawned and hatched, but reared to "smolt" size, 6 or 7 inches (15 to 18 cm) prior to being released. This process proved highly successful, and after a few years, adult chinook began to return to the river to spawn. Thus a natural cycle of salmon replenishment was established. The techniques employed at the Kalama River hatchery have since become the basis for commercial salmon ranching in many parts of the world.

Extensive salmon hatcheries that release young fish each year can be found in the United States, the Soviet Union, and Japan. Smaller-scale commercialization is found in Canada, Chile, France, Norway, and Sweden. The success experienced in these countries has prompted citizens of New Zealand and the Malvinas Islands (the Falklands) to try *their* hand at salmon ranching.

Japan releases a billion smolt into its rivers each spring. Following the river currents, the young salmon leave the mainland for ocean feeding grounds south of the Bering Sea, around the Aleutian Islands, and in the Gulf of Alaska. After feeding in these areas for three to five years, the grown fish return to the originating rivers, where they are harvested. During the fall of 1982, the Japanese harvest return was 28 million salmon, more than ten times greater than annual catches during the early 1900s.

Soviet ranchers release millions of pink and chum salmon each year into the streams of Sakhalin Island. During the past two years, the annual number of smolt released has been increased by 200 million. Current plans call for continued increases until, by the year 2000, 3 billion salmon smolt will be freed into Soviet Union streams each fall.

Feeding fish in a hatchery.

*Salmon eggs and young salmon at the stage
when the latter are called sac fry.*

Salmon ranching requires little in the way of feeding. It is estimated that only 1 percent of a salmon's growth is achieved while in captivity. Once released the salmon forages on its own. Ranchers, therefore, have exceedingly low feeding costs. The Japanese calculate that for every 2.2 pounds (1 kg) of young salmon released they get 176 pounds (80 kg) of adult fish.

At present, commercial ranching involves only the salmon. This does not mean that other species will not be adapted to ranching in the future. In the past, entrepreneurs saw salmon as a no-risk, high-yield investment.

A major conflict exists between the salmon rancher and small-scale fishing operations. Traditional fishing fleets face difficulty because of the large industrial activities of ranchers. At the same time, ranchers, who have already invested large sums in their operations, are losing potential profits because open-water fishing fleets harvest salmon before they enter the rivers where the catching pens of ranchers are located.

River pollution is another problem as hundreds of thousands of adult salmon pour into tiny streams that until commercial ranching began maintained only a small year-round trout population. Because of this, landowners, too, are protesting.

The sudden influx of salmon has caused sport fishers to invade rivers, often causing damage to private property. In some locations this problem is so dramatic that sport fishing has been banned in certain rivers.

NEW AREAS OF AQUACULTURE

While traditional aquaculture continues, new areas are being explored. Marine shrimp farming, for example, has become the fastest growing commercial aquaculture enterprise in the world. Because of the high market value of shrimp, millions of dollars have been invested into this area, and technology for culturing shrimp has developed rapidly.

Though cultivated in small numbers for centuries, lobster is now being studied for possible large-scale commercial harvesting. Despite the fact that lobsters spawn well in captivity, their low reproduction rate and slow growth—two to three years to reach marketable size—has made them so far an unfeasible crop. Another problem, and perhaps the most important one, is that young lobsters kill one another, causing large losses to the farmer. Because lobster supplies are low and demand—and therefore price—high, experiments to solve this problem and produce a species of fast-growing lobster continue.

CULTIVATION OF SEAWEED

One of the most interesting developments in the aquaculture field has been one brought about by Dr. Walter H. Adey, director of the Smithsonian Institution's Marine Science Laboratory. As a spin-off of research on coral reefs, Adey designed a floating-platform system that, through the continuous back-and-forth water motion over the structure's surface, creates a lawn-like growth of reef algae that is then cultivated, harvested, and taken ashore to be converted into methane, a colorless gas given off by organic matter as it decays. Among the many uses of this gas is the role it plays in the manufacture of many chemicals. Reef algae can be used to produce cheap alcohol as well as methane.

Growth rates of these floating algae gardens have reached 20 grams of dry weight per square meter a day. Until Adey's success, the highest recorded growth rate in the open ocean was 0.3 to 0.5 gram per square meter per day. Adey estimates that the productivity of his floating platforms could be increased further, by as much as 30 or 40 percent with moderate alterations.

This natural growing process can be easily adapted to open-ocean harvest, Adey says, if practical, large-scale harvesting devices can be designed and applied to miles of unused and unproductive open ocean without any polluting effects. Most critical, in our age of energy concerns, is that energy-consuming fertilization and cultivation will not be required.

For thousands of years human societies have utilized seaweed as a food source. Of the twenty-five thousand known seaweed species, seventy-five have been adapted in modern cuisines. Seaweed is both an excellent salad substitute and a fine "health" food. The blue-green algae that grow in both marine and freshwater habitats, for example, are 65 to 70 percent protein and also contain carbohydrates, minerals, and several essential vitamins.

Farmers have discovered that a number of land animals can also be nourished on an algae diet. Giant kelp, which grows 2 to 3 feet (60 to 90 cm) a day in open-water farms near California, is used to feed goats, sheep, and other livestock.

Countries in East Asia produce about 1 million tons of algae a year. The underwater algae and seaweed gardens in

Harvesting seaweed in Korea.

Japan, including one of the world's largest cultivations in Tokyo Bay, provide employment for more than half a million people.

Though Japan once led the world in seaweed farming, China is now the undisputed leader, particularly with species such as the abundant brown, cold-water kelp. Using methods developed by the Japanese after World War II, the Chinese cultivate young kelp plants in shallow tanks. Each fall the young plants are attached to buoyed ropes, where they grow up to 20 feet (6 m) before being harvested in the spring.

Commercial kelp operations in China, like the Qingdao Kelp Farm in the northern province of Shandong, harvest more than 150,000 tons a year. Of this, half is sold for alginates, which act as stabilizers and emulsifiers in medicines, food, and cosmetics. Through X-ray mutation and selective breeding, Chinese researchers are also attempting to produce strains of ocean kelp with a substantially higher iodine content to combat goiter, a common ailment in China.

AQUACULTURE PROBLEMS

Whether the crop be finfish, shellfish, crustaceans, algae or seaweed, the obstacles to aquaculture are many. Information about genetics, nutrition, and diseases of many species is lacking. Price fluctuations and the risk of failure deter investors. And a lack of coordination prevents the sharing of research.

Diseases are often encountered in aquaculture environments. Reared species are subject to hazardous parasitic, viral, bacterial, and fungal infections

Pollution and excess growths of algae and other vegetation along ocean coasts also create problems for saltwater cultures. One such problem is the red tide, whose name is taken from its color, caused by an overabundance of plant-like protozoa in the water. These protozoans produce a toxic substance that kills fish and other marine creatures.

Apart from problems of nature, productive aquaculture has caused economical and social problems. For example, the production of considerable tonnages of artificially reared fish could create downward pressure on market prices. If prices fall too low, many traditional fishers may be unable to compete and could be forced out of business. Prices that are too low, however, hurt others besides just the traditional fishers, since everyone involved in the fishing industry would eventually get less. The only winner when prices fall is the consumer.

Although fishers may not be the richest of individuals, together they make an important contribution to a nation's economy. In Southeast Asia, for example, some 6 million fishers (40 million if their families are added) contribute more than $2.6 billion to the economies of Hong Kong, Indonesia, Democratic Kampuchea, Malaysia, the Philippines, Singapore, Thailand, and the Socialist Republic of Vietnam. Similar figures can be found throughout the world. For this reason, and because they account for a large labor force, governments are listening to the complaints of traditional fishing enterprises regarding aquaculture competition.

Another human-related problem facing ocean farmers is that of competition from other forms of land and water use in coastal regions. Housing, tourism, and agriculture often maintain a higher level of priority than does the culturing of marine foods.

Nevertheless, world agencies such as the United Nations Development Programme and the Food and Agriculture Organization, the Consultative Group on International Agricultural Research, and the World Bank are all striving to solve these problems through international cooperation and the uniting of aquaculture research and technological knowledge. In the meantime, experts in engineering, physiology, nutrition, pathology, ecology, microbiology, feed technology, and economics are employed in the study of marine shrimp, freshwater prawn, crayfish, blue crab, brine shrimp, salmon and other finfish, oysters, clams, abalone, and scallops. Hybrid species that will resist various diseases as well as grow and reproduce more rapidly are being developed. New feeding technologies and vitamin-rich diets are cutting overhead costs while increasing harvest profits.

There is little doubt that farming of the sea will play a greater role as traditional ocean species are exploited. It is an area of constant development, an area in which the small-scale fishers, fish-farmer and aquatic plant culturalist must work side by side with industrial enterprises for both better harvests and better management of our ocean resources.

CHAPTER SIX

A SEA OF RESOURCES

The ocean is a repository of resources. Minerals and elements have accumulated in the sea for a billion years or more. Rivers carry chlorine and sulfur to the sea. Underwater volcanoes deposit boron and iodine along the ocean floor. Soil-laden waters carry calcium and silicon from weathered rock and eroding land down to the sea.

Although humankind has used some ocean minerals and elements for centuries, extracting them in sufficient quantities to meet today's needs would be an awesome task. Research is being carried out in many areas, however, in hopes of finding new and improved ways to harvest and utilize these resources.

Our great petroleum resource also had its origin in the sea, whether along the edges of the ocean, where once-submerged lands have risen, as in the Middle East and in the Gulf of Mexico, or in areas once covered by ancient inland seas, as in Oklahoma. In recent years, geologists have tapped the seafloor seeking oil deposits that might be held there. As a result, offshore wells are producing oil today off the coasts of Texas and Louisiana in the Gulf of Mexico and off California.

ELEMENTS

There are ninety-three naturally occurring elements on earth. Not to be confused with minerals, which contain a number of substances, elements cannot be broken down into anything simpler. A piece of pure gold, for example, consists only of the element gold. On the other hand, quartz may contain many elements, in different forms; thus it is a mineral.

Of the known elements, seventy-three currently can be found in some form in the world's oceans. In roughly 220,000 gallons (1 million liters) of seawater, for example, there are about 19,000 parts per million chlorine, 11,000 parts sodium, 1,300 parts magnesium, 884 parts sulfur, 400 parts calcium, 380 parts potassium, and 120 parts other compounds. Several of these substances, including iodine, bromine, and magnesium, are extracted from seawater for commercial use. Before any element is extracted, however, the need must be great enough to justify the investment of money and other resources.

A low percentage (0.006 percent) of the element iodine is present in the oceans. Yet, it is one of the most utilized natural resources of the sea. Iodine, an important medical antiseptic, is also used in photography. Some aquatic plants, such as algae, absorb and concentrate the iodine in seawater. Scientists calculate, for instance, that 20 tons (18,000 kg) of seawater contains 0.035 ounce (1 g) of iodine, which is concentrated into 7 ounces (200 g) of dry kelp. When processed, this iodine can be reclaimed from plants for commercial use. For this reason, seaweed is important to the chemical industry, though much of today's iodine is also obtained from saltpeter and oil-well brine.

Since 1933, large quantities of bromine, an important substance in the pharmaceutical and photographic industries and a component of high-octane gasoline, have also been derived from ocean sources. About half the bromine supply of the United States and 80 percent of the world's supply comes from the sea. Though great quantities are taken each year, this is one ocean resource that is plentiful. One cubic mile (4 cubic kilometers) of seawater, for example, can provide enough bromine to fill the needs of U.S. gasoline refineries for two years.

Another important element that comes from the sea is magnesium. In 1941, the Dow Chemical Company established a plant in Freeport, Texas, to extract magnesium from seawater.

Before it will release its magnesium, seawater must be treated in several stages with a number of chemicals. Although seawater contains only 0.13 percent magnesium, extraction from seawater is cheaper than from ore.

MINERAL RESOURCES

Ever since the scientific examination of the potato-sized nodules dredged by the HMS *Challenger* between 1872 and 1876, geologists have speculated about a richness of minerals on and in the seafloor. Today, a part of marine geology research is directed toward assessing these potential resources. Our knowledge of ocean minerals, with the exception of sea salts, has come about only during the past thirty years. We have glimpses of the magnitude of these resources but in reality have no true idea of how vast or scarce they actually are.

The seafloor contains several types of mineral resources. Most of these can be placed into one of six categories: construction materials, phosphorites, placer deposits, hydrothermal ore deposits, manganese nodules, and hydrocarbons.

CONSTRUCTION MATERIALS

Large deposits of sand, gravel, and limestone are exploited along much of the world's coastal waters. Though less exotic than other minerals, these common building materials are some of the most important and, in terms of quantity, most mined of all ocean resources. So vital are these resources, in fact, that the United States Geological Survey (USGS) has an ongoing program to locate and evaluate sand and gravel deposits throughout continental shelves of the nation's Exclusive Economic Zone.

Large quantities of sand are formed by organisms living in both shallow and deep water. In areas where sand does not exist, seashells that have been finely crushed by the ocean's waves are often used as sand substitutes in the production of cement.

The importance of ocean construction materials was demonstrated in Puerto Rico in 1972 when a citizen's committee reported to the government that the construction industry there would be facing a crisis by the end of the century if an adequate supply of sand were not secured within the next ten years. Researchers believe that the answer to this drastic need could very well be the ocean's sand resources. Already joint efforts of the USGS and the Department of Natural Resources of the Commonwealth of Puerto Rico have revealed offshore sand bodies whose exploitation would be worth an estimated $3.4 billion. This would fill the requirements of the nation's construction industry for over twenty years, based on current annual consumption.

Mining such construction materials as sand has some drawbacks. Considerations such as ocean currents and environmental impact can make underwater mining of sand, gravel, and similar resources an extremely complex matter. The removal of offshore deposits frequently contributes to the shifting of beach and inshore sand and could even cause coastal landslides. The underwater path of the resource and environmental setting of the deposits must therefore be studied with extreme care prior to exploitation.

PHOSPHORITES

Like the ocean's construction resources, phosphorite minerals are found in coastal waters, normally at depths of 300 to 1,000 feet (90 to 300 m).

While phosphorite minerals have many uses, they are most widely used for phosphate fertilizers. Off the coast of Southern California, phosphorite deposits amounting to 50 or 60 million tons are now being studied for their 30 percent phosphate content. If mined, these resources could be sold as fertilizer to all the West Coast states and many Asiatic nations bordering the Pacific.

Other large phosphorite resources are known to exist off the Republic of South Africa, southeastern United States, northwestern Africa, and western Australia. The fact that many land-based phosphate resources exist, however, limits the commercial interest in such marine deposits.

Ocean phosphorites include such elements as phosphorus and uranium. In some cases, these minerals are merely submerged continuations of land resources. In others, they are found on the seafloor in the form of nodules, grains, or slabs.

The formation of ocean phosphorites is governed by special conditions. Phosphorus, for example, is prominent in vertebrate bones and fish teeth. Since many marine species feed, live, and die in areas where aquatic vegetation such as algae is abundant, most phosphorus deposits have been located in these zones. It is still uncertain, however, whether the formation of phosphorites is entirely an inorganic process or if it also combines biological activities.

PLACER DEPOSITS

Placers are most commonly located along coastal areas in water depths of 300 feet (90 m) or less. A placer is a deposit of sand or gravel that contains minerals. Due to their easy access, placer deposits have been utilized by civilizations throughout history. The people of Southeast Asia found rich supplies of tin in such deposits, as did European populations. Despite this longtime use and the relatively simple recovery methods, much of the world's placers probably remain unexplored.

Most placers have been transported from land sources

Mineral deposits are often found near underwater vents (called "smoking chimneys" or just "smokers") like this.

and "placed" into the sea, usually a result of natural developments such as land shifts, volcanic activity, and glaciation from ancient ice ages. These mineral resources may contain several different elements, such as iron, gold, platinum, tin, zirconium, and titanium.

HYDROTHERMAL ORE DEPOSITS

Geologists believe that many valuable mineral deposits originate at seafloor-spreading ridges where hydrothermal —hot-water—vents are located. As the seafloor spreads, faults occur, providing conduits where cold seawater circulates downward into the hot crust. The water reacts with the hot rock, drawing from it elements such as maganese, zinc, silver, copper and to a lesser degree gold, iron, cadmium, and germanium. When the hot, mineral-laden water returns to the level of the seafloor, it shoots upward in a plume of minerals and forms chimneylike vents. Such dynamic geysers or "smokers" were photographed in 1979 from the Alvin, a submarine-like research vessel, along the hydrothermally active Galapagos spreading ridge.

Because many of these minerals have valuable applications in industry, from the production of jewelry to the manufacturing of transistors, studies are now underway in several parts of the world to determine the extent of these deposits and get a better understanding of how they are formed.

MANGANESE NODULES

For more than one hundred years the presence of potato-shaped manganese nodules on the seafloor has been known to scientists. What was not realized until recent years, however, was that these nodules represented a potentially important source of minerals.

Manganese nodules, which are believed to be of plant origin, are found at depths up to 13,000 feet (4 km) or more. The composition of most deep-sea nodules, including those recovered by the HMS *Challenger*, is about 24 percent manganese, 19 percent water, 14 percent iron; 2 percent cobalt, copper, and nickel, and 40 percent other elements. Maganese, iron, cobalt, and nickel are used in steel production, among other things.

Nearly 100 pounds of nodules per square yard (54 kilograms per square meter) are found in some parts of the Pacific, as well as in parts of the Atlantic and Indian Oceans. The U.S. Department of the Interior's Bureau of Mines has established a continuing Minerals Availability Program to collect and analyze information on such mineral resources and on their mining and processing. During the past seven years, data relating to manganese nodules have been gathered through the Scripps Institution of Oceanography and Washington State University, the U.S. Geological Survey, the National Oceanic and Atmospheric Administration, and several private consultants. Much raw information came from project DOMES (Deep Ocean Mining Environmental Study), sponsored by the National Oceanic and Atmospheric Administration. DOMES involved a detailed investigation of the marine atmosphere at three potential mine sites, and the determination of possible environmental effects of manganese-nodule mining.

Though studies continue, high costs may make mining of the DOMES project's mineral-rich nodules unfeasible unless the federal government is willing to assist private industry. "It is most likely that nodules will not be mined and processed in the foreseeable future without significant financial incentives," say U.S. Bureau of Mines investigators Burton B. Gosling and C. Thomas Hillman. "These incentives could be in the form of price supports, tax breaks, or other programs such as financing research and development."

MINING SEAFLOOR NODULES

Manganese nodules can be harvested in a number of ways. Conrad G. Welling and his colleagues at the Ocean Minerals

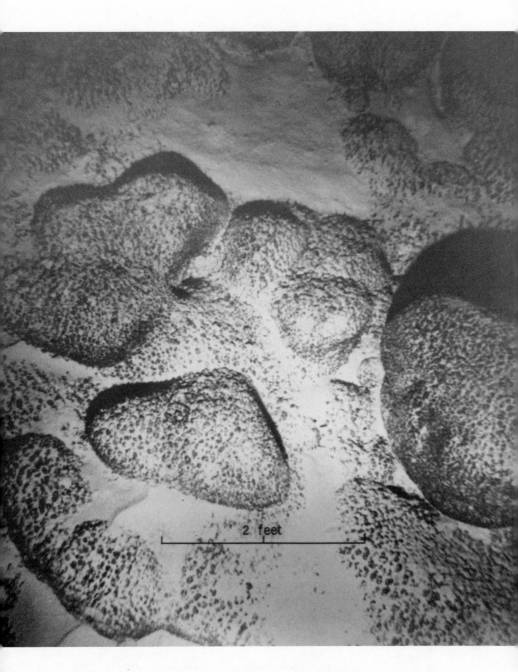

Manganese nodules on the seafloor.

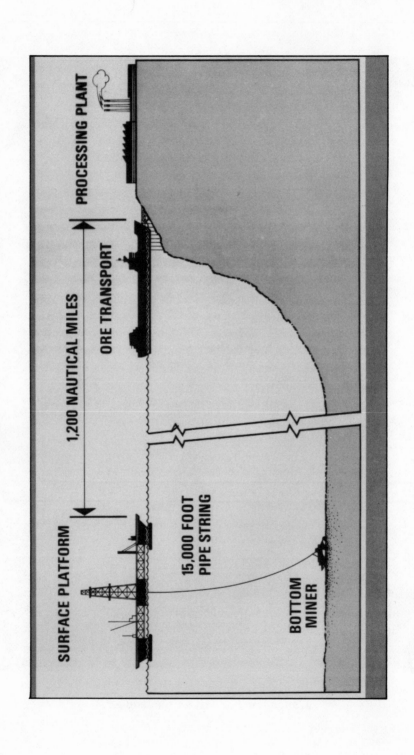

Company, one of four companies involved in ocean mining, have designed a surface-operated crawler system for collecting seafloor nodules.

In this system, a vehicle propelled across the bottom of the ocean does the actual mining. The nodules are picked up from the ocean floor by a rotating belt rake, then crushed, and finally pumped to the ship through a pipe. This system should enable the Ocean Minerals Company to dredge manganese nodules from depths as great as 16,000 feet (4.9 km).

Two other mining systems have also been tested somewhat successfully by the International Nickel Company and by Deepsea Ventures, two underwater mining pioneers. Other mining devices, including self-propelled rigs with closed-circuit television to aid in locating nodules, are being studied.

Long before an actual mining operation begins, the explored mine site is mapped, revealing the location of all bottom obstructions and specific mining blocks. Mining plans are drawn up at least one year in advance of the beginning of operations and take into consideration economics, licensing requirements, and other regulatory and environmental factors.

Major mining operations consist of twenty-hour days, three hundred days a year. Equipment modifications and repairs, including those that call for the removal of mining ships from the water, take place from late July, through August, and into part of September, when most major storms occur.

Ships tow the mining device at an average speed of 1 mile (about 2 km) per hour. Once nodules have been collected and pumped to the ship, they go through a series of

A manganese nodule mining and processing system.

washings. The raw nodules are then transported to shore terminals where they undergo additional treatment prior to being pumped to processing plants, some as far as 25 miles (40 km) away.

At processing plants, such as the Cuprous plant on the United States West Coast, ore is crushed and, through a number of processes, elements extracted.

The key factor narrowing the marine-mineral industry's expansion is financial. Initial research and development budgets for manganese-nodule mining may cost civilian and government agencies more than $150 million. To mine and process ore, once located, requires nearly $2 billion from businesses involved. This includes such factors as the cost of mining ships, equipment, buildings, transportation, and labor.

Due to the need for such large financial outlays, ocean-floor mining is generally limited to large international businesses, such as Standard Oil Company of Ohio. Oil companies, in fact, have shown great interest in ocean mining and may play a major role in its future.

HYDROCARBON RESOURCES

The richest and most commercialized of all ocean mineral deposits are the hydrocarbons. These are compounds consisting of only carbon and hydrogen. More than 22 percent of the world's petroleum and much of its natural gas are obtained from these marine resources.

Petroleum and natural gas deposits are generally restricted to ancient basins where hydrocarbons have been forming for over millions of years. Because land shifts often occur along ocean shelves, finding such basins is extremely difficult.

Though some early attempts were made at tapping the oceans' oil resources, successful drilling technology did not come about until 1946.

Today modern platform rigs are used in the Black Sea, the Gulf of Mexico, the Arctic Sea, the North Sea, the Sulu Sea in the Philippines, and off the coast of California. On offshore oil platforms such as Mobil Oil Company's Statfjord "B" in the North Sea drilling takes place as far as 22,000 feet (6.7 km) below the ocean floor. The Statfjord "B" is located 100 miles (160 km) off the coast of Norway in about 470 feet (140 m) of water.

Within the Statfjord "B," a core structure eight stories high with two seven-story wings provides living quarters for a crew of two hundred. More than eleven thousand man-years went into the platform, which cost $1.8 billion to build. Mobil Oil considers the money well spent, however, considering the fact that the Statfjord "B" has a pumping output of 150,000 barrels of oil per day.

Offshore oil platforms similar to the Statfjord "B" are under construction or already operating in much of the world. Billions of dollars each year are earned by private industries involved in the extraction of offshore oil and gas resources. At the same time, many ocean-bordering nations have been able to increase their own revenues through Outer Continental Shelf Leasing programs.

OUTER CONTINENTAL SHELF LEASING

Because most coastal nations of the world have made their claim to Exclusive Economic Zones (EEZ) extending 200 nautical miles (over 370 km) seaward of their shorelines, industries wishing to search for and extract ocean resources in those areas must first obtain proper government authorization. In most cases, this involves the purchase of a lease that allows them the rights to specific resources in a given location over a determined period of time. Therefore, not only the industry but also the government profits from the ocean's marketable deposits.

Many of the economic benefits of Outer Continental Shelf (OCS) Leasing programs are quite obvious; others are less obvious. In the United States, OCS funds have been used to purchase federal, state, and local parklands, endangered-species habitats, and recreational areas. Jobs have been created not only for those working on offshore projects, but those involved in supporting these operations. In Louisiana, offshore activities in 1981 supported 125,000 people and generated household earnings of more than $1.8 billion.

Increasing recognition of these facts has resulted in more active support for OCS leasing from labor and consumer groups throughout the world. There are still many, however, who feel we are treading in unknown areas when it comes to ocean resources. Some say that we know too little about the long-range effects mining and offshore drilling will have on the environment. Though oil spills have caused extreme problems to marine wildlife in recent years, the U.S. Department of Interior argues that the 1969 Santa Barbara oil spill remains the only one, in the course of drilling more than thirty thousand wells in the nation's EEZ, that resulted in significant amounts of oil reaching shore.

A study on the effects of oil spills carried out near the Woods Hole Oceanographic Institution in Massachusetts demonstrated, however, that blowouts and spills had long-lasting biological effects that covered much greater areas than anyone had previously expected. The reason for this is that most experts considered the surface area covered by oil to be the limit of the oil's damage. In reality, a considerably larger area was affected by oil residues carried in underwater currents and deposited onto bottom sediment.

*Offshore oil rigs can
be found throughout
the world.*

"Today we are seeing an assault on our Outer Continental Shelf, including pressures for such activities as oil and gas development [and] seabed mining," explains Congresswoman Barbara Boxer, who holds positions on the subcommittee on Oceanography and House committee on Merchant Marine and Fisheries. "Can the oceans absorb this stress and increased pollution? How many species extinctions and population shifts can be sustained by the ocean without causing dramatic consequences? The answer is, we simply do not know."

FRESHWATER FROM
THE SEA

In addition to minerals, one of the most important ocean resources is freshwater. Large-scale conversion of saltwater to freshwater has far-reaching implications for the world. It is estimated that each day more than 1.25 billion gallons (4.7 billion liters) of freshwater are already being produced in plants that remove salt from seawater. This process is known as "desalination." In areas such as Israel, where pure water is scarce, desalination could change the appearance of the land, making it green. Already many Middle East nations are benefiting from desalination plants located there.

Forty-four plants able to desalinize 25,000 gallons (95,000 liters) or more per day were constructed between 1968 and 1970, bringing the world total to 686. Today more operations have been added, and output capacities have increased greatly. The desalination plant in Rosanta, Mexico, for instance, produces 7.5 million gallons (28 million liters) per day. One of Europe's largest plants, located in Terneuzen, Netherlands, has a capacity of 7.6 million gallons (29 million liters) per day. The Soviet Union maintains a large desalination plant at Schevelenko, with an estimated output of 32 million gallons (120 million liters) of freshwater each day.

When salt is removed from seawater by drying in the sun, the scene might look like this one in California.

Evaporation is not the only means of removing salt from seawater. In fact, we now process seawater by reverse osmosis, passing it under pressure through a membrane. By this method, salt stays behind and freshwater comes out the opposite side of the membrane.

Why is freshwater conversion important? First, it can provide freshwater to areas where such water is scarce. Second, it can provide supplementary natural water where supplies are normally sufficient but drop periodically due to extreme heat or drought. Of additional importance, freshwater conversion plants with large production capabilities may someday be called upon to fill part of our daily water needs as more freshwater supplies become contaminated through various pollutants.

MARINE GEOLOGY

Locating and studying the sea's mineral resources is one of the tasks of the marine geologist. Early pioneers relied on simple devices to aid them in ocean research. Today marine geologists maintain an array of sophisticated instruments and underwater vehicles to find and recover the oceans' resources.

Most of the tools and methods used to study the ocean floors were invented and developed within the last half century. In this regard, marine geology is still a relatively young science, with many unexplored frontiers.

Direct observation of the seafloor is difficult and time consuming. Sophisticated research vessels and oceanographic instrumentation have made the job easier. The United States Geological Survey currently uses from twelve to fifteen ships of various sizes, and from these floating laboratories marine geologists deploy their instruments.

A simple and rapid method of exploring the seafloor from a ship employs a long metal pipe weighted at the top to drive into the ocean bottom to obtain samples. This method is called *coring*.

The pipe is attached to a long cable and allowed to fall to the bottom where it picks up substances, called sediments, on the ocean floor. It is then pulled up and the sediments removed, in long strips. Data from core samples obtained by this method can provide much information about the earth's recent geologic history, as well as reveal the mineral content of the seafloor.

Several new types of marine research vehicles have been developed that are proving to be valuable tools for marine geologic studies. They allow scientists to descend beneath the water to observe and sample the seafloor. A small *submersible* vehicle can carry one navigator and one scientist, but some larger ones, operating as much as 6,000 feet (2,000 m) below the ocean's surface, carry a five-person crew. The deepest oceanic trenches at depths exceeding 7 miles (11 km) have already been visited by these vessels.

One of the most noted deepwater vehicles is the Alvin, operated by the Woods Hole Oceanographic Institution. To dislodge rock samples, the Alvin has mechanical arms. Cameras, water samplers, and other instruments are used to collect samples, including seafloor sediments and mineral deposits.

In 1968, the National Science Foundation initiated a worldwide investigation of the seafloor called the Deep Sea Drilling Project (DSDP). Using technology developed by the petroleum industry, DSDP ships—in particular the *Glomar Challenger*—drilled and recovered extensive core sections, some more than a mile (1.6 km) long, from the ocean floor. This research provided governments and industries with an overall picture of much of the world's ocean resources.

In the search for oil and gas deposits, geologic research is extremely important because it provides a sophisticated means of gathering data about the ocean floor. Tests called seismic surveys use reflected sound waves to obtain valuable information about the shape and thickness of the seafloor as well as about what lies below it. Seismic surveys can

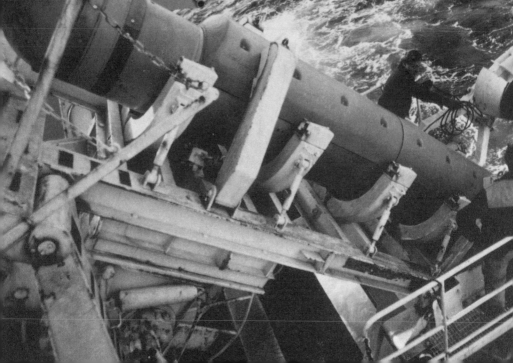

also locate oil and gas deposits commonly found trapped in deep accumulations of rocks.

For seismic surveys, sound waves are sent out. When they come in contact with an object, they reflect a signal. The reflected signals are printed on moving chart paper to create a graphic profile, or cross section, revealing the layers of the seafloor. The profiles are recorded with great clarity and in many cases show structures as deep as 6 miles (10 km) beneath the ocean bottom.

Another method of charting the ocean floor is called side-scan sonar. Beams of sound are sent sideways from the ship's course to map the seafloor. Irregularities on the bottom alter the energy in the signal bounced back to the receiver, and these irregularities are used to produce a picture of the ocean floor.

During the summer of 1984, the entire western United States from Canada to Mexico was surveyed using the sophisticated side-scan sonar system instrument with the acronym GLORIA.

Developed in England, GLORIA is towed behind a research vessel and is capable of surveying patches as wide as 38 miles (60 km) in a single pass. This large survey width, coupled with GLORIA's fast survey speed, allows as much as 10,000 square miles (26,000 square kilometers) to be mapped in a single day. The 1984 project, conducted in cooperation with the United Kingdom's Institute of Oceanographic Sciences, was extremely valuable in determining the presence of, as well as the potential for, economic resources, including oil and gas, cobalt-rich crusts, maganese crusts, sand and gravel, and phosphates.

Above: *the research submarine* Alvin.
Below: GLORIA, *a sophisticated instrument for surveying the ocean floor.*

Today, nations are joining in cooperative marine geology programs. By combining the expertise of the many marine scientists around the world, we can expand our understanding of the oceans and ultimately appraise the extent of all the resources that lie beneath their surface.

CHAPTER SEVEN

ENERGY FROM THE OCEAN

For centuries, human beings have utilized the energy of the ocean for a variety of purposes. The ancient Egyptians harnessed sea power by building mills that operated with the rising and falling of the tides. Similar mills were used by early European civilizations. In the United States in the early seventeenth century, Dutch settlers constructed such mills near New York.

Today power plants driven by surging tides are operated in France, the Soviet Union, and China. Each plant provides an annual average of 500 million kilowatt-hours of electricity, enough to supply the power needs of a community of ninety thousand people. Canada, too, is looking to harness the ocean's tidal energy with a $6 billion tidal hydroelectric dam project for Nova Scotia's Bay of Fundy. But the search for ways to use ocean power does not stop here. Now being designed are large floating turbines, windmills, and other devices to convert the ocean's energy to electricity.

WAVE POWER

There is enormous energy in the ocean tides, waves, and currents. A single 4-foot (1.2-m) wave lasting ten seconds, for example, expends more than 35,000 horsepower for every mile (1.6 km) of coastline it strikes.

One of the simplest, yet most promising, attempts to harness wave energy to date is a cement structure being tested along the coast of Algeria, in Africa. The structure consists of a large reservoir built into the shore and two walls extending outward into the sea in a V-shape. Waves enter the wide front of the structure and are funneled toward the narrow end of the V, where they spill into the reservoir. The constant outward flow of this great volume of water from the reservoir operates turbines that convert the energy into electricity.

While this energy-producing device works, it operates only when there are sufficiently large waves of fairly uniform size, which are necessary to drive enough water through to provide a steady-enough flow of reservoir water to work the turbines. Without such waves, the operation ceases to function. It is therefore an unreliable source of electricity.

TAMING THE TIDES

Unlike waves, ocean tides are reliable. Twice a day on the western side of Nova Scotia, for instance, tide water from the Atlantic Ocean rushes into the 60-mile- (100-kilometer-) long Bay of Fundy with a physical force equal to that generated by the engines of 8,000 freight locomotives. In the Minas Basin, a tiny upper section of the Bay, as much as 6.5 million cubic feet (184 million cubic meters) of water enters or exits every second—a flow ten times greater than that of the Mississippi River into the Gulf of Mexico. For this and other reasons, the Minas Basin has been selected as the site for a new tidal hydroelectric dam.

Since 1910, engineers have entertained the idea of harnessing the Bay of Fundy's tidal power. Until 1976, though, the more than 200-foot- (60-m-) high, 5-mile- (8-km-) long dam, which would stand as tall as a fourteen-story building and contain 128 turbines, was merely a dream. In that year, with dramatic jumps in world oil prices and the increasing need for safe, clean energy without the potential radiation hazards of nuclear power plants, the Tidal Power Corporation of Nova Scotia began planning one of the world's largest dams, a project that would produce almost 5,000 megawatts of power, more than three times the output of the Colorado River Hoover Dam and enough power to provide more than 7.5 million homes with electricity.

A number of problems have delayed the Bay of Fundy project. Now, however, the technical problems have been solved, money is available, and there is a growing need for the electricity.

The dam's turbines would operate an average of twelve hours each day. When the tide rises, water would pass through an opening below the dam. Once the water has reached its peak level, a gate would close the opening. Then, as the tide recedes, water would be forced through a power-house, where it works turbines, generating electricity.

The extremely simple and reliable dam would provide clean, safe, cheap electricity in quantities sufficient to supply citizens as far as Boston and New York City, a distance of nearly 600 miles (almost 1,000 km). The dam would not only fill the energy needs of Nova Scotia, but bring in revenue from United States consumers. In addition, the Fundy project would insure jobs and economic development in an underdeveloped section of Canada.

At the same time, there are potential problems with the dam's construction. The Canadian Wildlife Service believes that several species of migratory birds could be killed when their mud-flat feeding grounds are flooded as a result of the dam's blocking the water. They are also concerned that several fish species could be killed by being passed through the turbines, damaging commercial and sport fishing as far south as Florida.

According to some, the dam might devastate the entire

American shad fishing industry. Even if the actual kill rate were only 20 percent, Michael Dadswell, a Canadian fisheries biologist, believes the shad fishing as far south as Georgia and Florida would be dramatically affected.

The tides, too, could be disrupted. Because of the dam facade, tides in certain areas could increase, flooding private property. Scientific investigators have even speculated that the dam could alter tidal patterns as far south as Boston. In addition to flooding farmlands and towns, Portland, Maine's largest city, might even have to reconstruct its entire sewage system.

For these reasons, the Tidal Power Corporation is moving slowly and studying closely the consequences of producing Canada's tidal hydoelectric dam. Organizations involved in the Bay of Fundy project are cooperatively working to find proper and safe methods to exploit the ocean tides.

THERMAL ENERGY

A power source that may one day be important the world over is thermal energy, in which the difference in temperature between the ocean's warm surface water and the cold water 1.5 miles (2.4 km) below is used to drive an electric generating turbine that floats on the surface. Ironically, the idea behind the recovery of this energy was documented more than one hundred years ago by the French physician and physicist Jacques d'Arsonval. At that time d'Arsonval's idea was of little interest since neither the technology nor the need for such energy existed. Today, the need to exploit this untapped energy source does exist, and the technology has now been developed to do so.

In 1930, Georges Glaude, with the support of the French government, took the idea that his countryman had documented in the late 1800s and constructed the first thermal-energy conversion operation off Matanzas Bay, Cuba. Glaude built the plant on land, where it drew warm surface water from the bay and used it to evaporate sea-water in a vacuum. The resulting steam drove a turbine. Simultaneously, cold water drawn through a 2-mile- (1.6-km-) long tube that extended 2,000 feet (609 m) below the ocean surface cooled the steam in the plant's condensers.

Though the tiny power plant did in fact work, the energy used to drive the many pumps needed to maintain a vacuum powerful enough to draw the necessary water was greater than the energy produced. Before the problem could be rectified, a storm destroyed the plant, along with Glaude's hopes of obtaining "thermal" electricity from the ocean.

After carefully studying the early French project, the United States Department of Energy and the National Oceanic and Atmospheric Administration (NOAA) began the Ocean Thermal Energy Conversion (OTEC) project to assist the efforts of private industry to harness this un-tapped source of power.

In July 1981, NOAA's Office of Ocean Minerals and Energy established regulations to clear the way for U.S. industry to become involved in this new technology, hoping that big business would find OTEC a profitable venture.

According to James Lawless, then acting director of NOAA's Office of Ocean Minerals and Energy, "Although it is unlikely that there will be any large OTEC power plants installed off the U.S. mainland in the immediate future, use of OTEC on U.S. islands and export of OTEC technology to only a small percentage of the countries where oceanic conditions make OTEC feasible could result in more than $200 billion in American business between now and the year 2010. The effect on the domestic economy—about 144,000 new jobs and $780 million in tax revenues annually—would be salutary indeed."

A Department of Energy study indicates that more than sixty nations, lying roughly 20 degrees north and south of the equator, have the coastal water conditions needed to make OTEC economically feasible—a temperature difference between deep cold water and warm surface water of at least 40 degrees Fahrenheit (4.5°C). In 1979, the Lockheed company, in partnership with the Dillingham Corporation, the Swedish Alfa-Level Company, and the State of Hawaii, based a three-month experimental floating OTEC plant off Hawaii's coast at a cost of $3 million. The miniplant was designed to produce fifty kilowatts of electricity during its sea trial, forty of which were to run the plant. The operation worked to perfection. Not only was power produced, but OTEC technology was demonstrated to be feasible as well as economically competitive. From this study, the Department of Energy speculates that OTEC-generated electric power may be competitive with fossil fuel power on certain tropical islands and coastal nations. In fact, the Energy Department predicts that OTEC energy on some islands could cost 43 percent less than conventional electricity by 1995.

The United States is not alone in the field of OTEC research. Japan's Kyushu Electric Power Co. is now constructing a small plant to locate near Okinawa, where it will use the discharge of a nearby oil-fired plant as its source of hot water. The OTEC plant will provide a net output of fifty kilowatts.

Larger plants with capacities of several thousand kilowatts are foreseen by the executives of Kyushu Electric if the current OTEC operations are successful. This would ease Japan's concern over high imported-oil costs and the expense of providing electricity to thirty distant island communities.

When one considers the fact that one 400-megawatt OTEC facility would be capable of producing enough

Illustration of an OTEC plant off the coast of Hawaii, cut away to show the underwater workings.

power for sixty thousand households, saving 2 million tons of coal or 6 million barrels of oil each year, it is easy to understand why there is such a growing interest in the OTEC program. The question now is whether industry is willing to make long-term financial commitments to the OTEC program.

Following the success of its mini-OTEC plant in Hawaii, Lockheed moved ahead with designs for several future operations. Already on the drawing boards are possible OTEC facilities configured for shipboard, ocean-shelf-mounted, and land-based operations. By far the most sophisticated of the Lockheed designs is that of a gigantic floating heat engine, similar in appearance to a modern space lab. The plant is conceived on such a large scale, in fact, that it will allow technicians actually to work within the OTEC center, just as astronauts would work in specially designed space bases.

THE PROBLEMS AND FUTURE OF OTEC

The OTEC project is not without problems, however. The most significant barrier is the high cost of manufacturing a productive plant, whether on land or sea. By some estimates such a plant would cost more than $1 billion.

Other obstacles include corrosion, degradation, and the lack of backup systems in the event of unforeseen damage or repairs. All objects are subject to extensive corrosion and degradation. Ships, for example, work on a planned cycle whereby their schedule allows for their removal from the sea for repairs neccessitated by exposure to such substances as ordinary saltwater. High waves and winds also present a potential hazard to energy plants located in open waters. Because projected OTEC plants are extremely large and backup units may not always be available, a cycle system such as that used by ocean-going vessels may not be feasible. This is a hurdle that must be overcome. Should a workable plan not be devised, entire cities may be without energy if a major malfunction ever occurred at the main plant.

Even if these barriers are overcome, there remains the problem of long-range transfer of power from the producing plant to energy storage centers. At least one company in the United States is now testing such power transfers.

Some companies are also experimenting with combined OTEC and desalinization units. Through such plants, either floating or shore based, large-scale conversion of saltwater to freshwater would take place using the OTEC evaporation system. At the same time, a turbine would be driven by the steam, creating electrical power. Uniting these systems to produce freshwater and electricity simultaneously would in the long run lower production costs and increase profits. Other combined projects that would produce electricity and alcohol, or food are also in the planning stages.

CHAPTER EIGHT

THE OCEAN AND COMMERCIAL WASTE

Ever since the industrial revolution, in the eighteenth century, hazardous wastes have been transported for direct discharge into the ocean. For a long time, few people were concerned about the effects this might have on the marine environment. But as time passed, it became increasingly clear that if such dumping continued, many of the ocean's natural resources would be damaged, possibly permanently destroyed.

For this reason, marine pollution has become a subject of international concern. At the London Dumping Convention, held in 1972, guidelines were established under the Prevention of Marine Pollution by Dumping of Wastes and Other Matter Act by ninety-two contributing nations, including the United States, to regulate ocean dumping of materials that might have an adverse impact on human health or the marine environment. The dumping of commercial waste also became a major topic of discussion in the negotiations of the United Nations Law of the Sea agreement. This treaty, ratified in 1982, required that all participating nations take necessary measures to prevent, reduce, and control all sources of pollution to the ocean, including the dumping of toxic substances.

The United States did not sign the Law of the Sea treaty. However, here, as in several European countries, rigid guidelines have been established regarding industrial dumping of wastes into the ocean. The U.S. Environmental Protection Agency's Ocean Dumping Criteria, in fact, called for a complete phaseout of chemical dumping in the oceans by the end of 1981. Though court decisions delayed the enforcement of this deadline, many industries stopped dumping by 1982, and others were issued special limited permits that enabled them to continue dumping while arranging for the switch over to alternative methods of waste disposal.

Industry has sought to develop ways to reduce its need for toxic materials and ways to recycle those materials already used, while new methods for the safe disposal of more than 450 products labeled hazardous by the Environmental Protection Agency (EPA) are found. Obvious to everyone, however, are the limitations under which researchers are working.

In the United States alone, 260 million tons of new hazardous waste are generated each year, in addition to all the waste now in storage. It has to go somewhere. There are three options: air, land, and water. Government and industry both agree that the ocean is the best "receptacle" for disposal of certain materials.

"The ocean can and should play a role in the management of society's wastes," says Kenneth S. Kamlet, director of the Pollution and Toxic Substances Division of the National Wildlife Federation. "But it is wrong to assume that persistent toxic materials can be harmlessly assimilated by the simple expedient of dilution." In other words, dispersing toxic materials in large quantities of saltwater does not necessarily make them any less hazardous.

Government and industry are therefore working on safe

methods of transporting and disposing of toxic wastes. According to many experts, ocean incineration is the answer for materials such as polychlorinated biphenyl compounds (PCBs).

PCBs include several industrial lubricants and fluids. They are extremely poisonous and resist decomposition in water and soil, posing a long-term threat to both nature and humankind.

OCEAN INCINERATION

Ocean incineration refers to the disposal method in which certain hazardous wastes are transported aboard specially designed ships to the open sea, where they are pumped into extremely high-temperature incinerators and vaporized. What remains of the substances then escapes into the air through the ship's smokestacks. This system of disposal has been commercially used in Europe since 1969. Since that time more than 100,000 tons (per year) of liquid hazardous wastes have been incinerated at a burn site in the North Sea.

In 1974, at the request of Shell Oil Company in Houston, the EPA initiated a series of research burns aboard the incinerator ship *Vulcanus*. The nation's stockpile of Agent Orange, the deadly defoliant used in Vietnam, was successfully incinerated at sea during these tests. The most recent research burns were conducted in 1982, during which PCBs were successfully incinerated with destruction efficiencies of 99.9999 percent. This means that only 0.0001 percent of the hazardous waste remained after incineration.

At first glance this may seem impressive. When the total amounts are calculated, however, this means that tons of PCBs enter the atmosphere and ocean unburned. For example, 0.0001 percent of the total liquid hazardous waste incinerated each year in the North Sea is 10 tons (9,000 kg). Using these figures, incineration of the United State's annual hazardous wastes would account for the dispersing of an estimated 26,000 tons of potentially dangerous material into the environment.

In September 1980, an Interagency Ad-Hoc work Group, composed of representatives of the EPA, the U.S. Maritime Administration, the National Bureau of Standards, and the U.S. Coast Guard, reported on their evaluation of incineration of hazardous waste at sea. They concluded that incineration at sea aboard specially designed or modified ships has been demonstrated to be an environmentally acceptable and efficient means for the destruction of certain liquid, hazardous, organic chemical wastes.

There are those, however, who disagree. Many experts feel that more studies are required, arguing that too little is known about the influence incineration residue may have on marine environments. Already as a result of waste dumping, low-level toxic contamination has become a problem even in deep-water species. Researchers in Southern California recently found that a dump site off Malibu, in water 200 feet (about 60 m) deep, contained seriously contaminated fish. A similar search from Port San Luis south to Ensenada, Mexico, and out 90 miles (over 140 km) to the Cortez Bank failed to turn up any uncontaminated fish.

At the same time, government agencies are being pressured by industry to move ahead. In a May 1985 edition of *The Houston Port*, for example, an editorial regarding burning of hazardous wastes at sea concluded that: "No one says it is the perfect answer. But it seems to be the best among several choices. If at-sea incineration isn't the best available solution, let opponents suggest a better one. If it is, let's get on with it."

In two studies released by the EPA in April 1985 it was revealed that (1) demand for commercial incineration will soon be seven and one-half times greater than existing landfill capacity; (2) utilizing the now-available incinerator ship *Apollo One* could nearly double current commercial capacity and offset 30 percent of the anticipated shortfall; (3) land-based incineration is thirty to forty times more risky to human health than ocean incineration; (4) due to advanced radar, double-hull construction, and increased maneuverability, today's ocean incinerator ship is fifty thousand times less likely to cause a spill than other types of vessels carrying hazardous cargo.

Although no harmful effects on human health or the marine environment have been reported as a result of commercial test burns, some experts feel that inadequate burning could result in the creation of certain forms of dioxin (one ingredient of Agent Orange) and other materials that are more deadly than the original toxic wastes which we are trying to dispose of. Critics also point out that the mere transporting of these materials is a risk factor. They say that spills at sea are extremely difficult to clean up, increasing the risk of poisoning marine life, upsetting the balance of the sea, and ultimately harming people.

Another reason that many of the groups involved are pushing for marine disposal of toxic wastes is that the ocean is a common source. Unlike the land, the ocean is not protected with the same force of public outrage and legal recourse that protects private property. If someone were to propose dumping toxic wastes on land, nearby residents would be expected to protest. And elected officials will generally support these protests. The ocean, on the other hand—once one gets beyond the coastal areas—is nobody's backyard, and fish do not vote. According to some people, if disposal decisions are based on social and political influences, the ocean will always lose out.

Some argue that the ocean, like the atmosphere, should not be used for the disposal of hazardous materials such as persistent synthetic chemicals, pesticides, and PCBs, because it is a dispersal rather than containment medium. In other words, pollutants placed into the ocean spread across miles of open water, whereby land disposal isolates and contains such wastes.

There is much controversy about the possibility of incineration at sea as a means of disposal. On one side, industry sees it as a quick and relatively safe means to rid themselves of many tons of waste now stored as well as future waste. For years, the land and sea were their outlets for such waste. Now legislation has forced them to find alternative disposal sources that meet tight environmental restrictions. They feel they have found such a source in at-sea incineration and that the government's nonapproval is merely wasting their time and costing them money.

On the other hand, many environmental groups and government agencies feel it is foolhardy and wrong to assume that what we do not know cannot hurt us, or that, if unanticipated problems arise, science will be able to remedy them after they have occurred. Equally, they feel it is wrong to endorse ocean dumping merely because it is convenient and "appears" to rid society of the problem, when in reality the consequences have not been evaluated against those of other disposal alternatives.

Opposition or no, the U.S. Maritime Administration has guaranteed loans of $55 million to At-Sea Incineration Corporation of Port Newark, New Jersey, for the construction of the *Apollo Two*, a modern incineration ship designed after its sister, the *Apollo One*.

THE *APOLLO*

One-third longer than a football field, the *Apollo One* was designed to burn a variety of liquid wastes, such as pesticides, benzene, and PCBs. The ship can carry over 1 million gallons (5 million liters) of hazardous waste in its twelve isolated cargo tanks. The liquid is constantly monitored by means of a sophisticated computer sonar system to further insure safe handling of toxic materials.

Once at sea, the crew of the *Apollo* pumps waste into two incinerators located at the rear of the ship. Nitrogen, a gas that lessens the chance of fire or explosion, fills the cargo tanks as the waste is removed. Should the waste ignite while being transferred to the incinerators, chemical foam to smother the flames would be released automatically from compartments at the top of each tank.

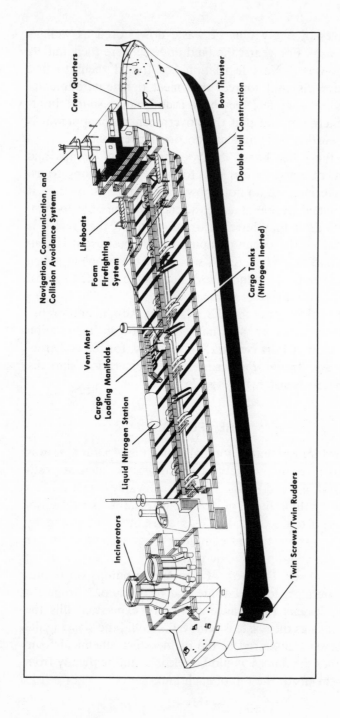

Crew Quarters

Navigation, Communication, and
Collision Avoidance Systems

Lifeboats

Foam
Firefighting
System

Vent Mast

Cargo
Loading Manifolds

Liquid Nitrogen Station

Incinerators

Bow Thruster

Double Hull Construction

Cargo Tanks
(Nitrogen Inerted)

Twin Screws/Twin Rudders

*Drawing of the Apollo, a ship designed
for burning and dumping wastes at sea.*

Inside the incinerators, wastes are sprayed into combustion chambers with high-pressure nozzles. These chambers have been heated to 2,300 degrees Fahrenheit (1,300°C). The intense heat oxidizes toxic materials such as PCBs to a vapor composed of water, carbon dioxide, and hydrogen chloride, a powerful acid. At this stage, the compound is still hazardous. Soon after the vapors escape through the *Apollo*'s smokestacks and settle into the sea, they become neutralized by the sea water.

WHERE TO BURN?

To further ensure the safety of marine and human environments, most countries using or intending to use at-sea incineration to solve their industrial waste problems have established specific zones for commercial ocean burning.

"When we examine a site, we look at several things," explains EPA's Assistant Administrator for Water, Jack E. Ravin. "First of all, how busy is the site? We do not want to pick a location where a number of other activities are already underway. Second, we are looking at the depth of waters, and what might happen to the material in final deposition at the site. The air and ocean currents are important. . . ."

Air currents are, naturally, a principal factor in determining how far toxic vapors will travel before settling. Ocean currents play a major role in regard to where such vapors are dispersed. Though the burn site currently being used in the North Sea is only 50 to 225 feet (15 to 70 m) deep, greater depths are believed to provide a higher safety factor. For this reason, the proposed North Atlantic burn site, to be used by the United States, ranges in depth from 4,000 to 5,000 feet (1,200 to 1,500 m).

Whether deeper water truly provides a higher level of safety is hard to determine at this early stage. However, as pointed out earlier, studies indicate that even at great depths, fish have become contaminated by toxic wastes.

Another U.S. burn site is located in the Gulf of Mexico, and a proposal has been drafted for the establishment of a third site off the Florida-Georgia coast.

MARINE TRANSFER TERMINALS

In 1980, the Chemical Control Corporation of Elizabeth, New Jersey, exploded and burned, releasing a number of hazardous substances into the atmosphere. A much more deadly catastrophe took place in December 1984 when a gas leak occurred at a Union Carbide plant in Bhopal, India. Incidents such as these have brought worldwide attention to the handling and storage of dangerous industrial wastes.

The marine terminals used for the storage and transfer of toxic wastes to ships are a major part of the commercial ocean incineration program. The transfer facilities have been designed to address a variety of technical matters, including construction materials, foundation design, and instrumental selection. All waste-storage containers are protected by a spill-containment system, including concrete dikes capable of holding the entire contents of a storage tank should it ever leak.

In addition to the spill-prevention system, each tank has special safety features, including computer-assisted level monitors that automatically stop the intake of waste once the container is full; an oxygen-free atmosphere, which reduces the risk of fire or explosions; and a fire-prevention system that extends through the storage tanks, tanker trucks, and piping network.

If, despite the safety systems, a fire should occur inside one of the storage tanks, a compartment will automatically release an extinguishing foam blanket on the entire contents of the tank.

Even with such safety features, the construction of marine transfer facilities in Port Newark, New Jersey, and Lake Charles, Louisiana, has met with some government opposition. Hearings on the permit applications have drawn large crowds and citizen protests. While many of the complaints were more emotional than scientific, governmental agencies have listened. The EPA's Scientific Advisory Board believes there is potential danger in the development of an operation where relatively little research data exist. Many environmental groups believe that the construction of such sites and burning of wastes at sea would only encourage industries to generate more toxic wastes rather than provide incentives to stem their production.

There are some advantages to building waste-transfer facilities in these two locations, other than the mere fact that they offer ocean access. New Jersey and nearby New York, for example, generate enormous quantities of hazardous materials, primarily because of their industrialized economy. Many of these waste producers are small operations that cannot afford to build on-site treatment facilities and instead look for other ways to dispose of their wastes.

Similarly, Texas and Louisiana host many of the nation's largest hazardous-waste-producing industries, such as the Shell Oil Company. Locating waste-transfer facilities along the Gulf of Mexico coast would eliminate long overland transfers of wastes.

Municipal health officials in many coastal cities where such facilities have been proposed warn that approval would clear the roads for large amounts of hazardous materials to pass through some of the nation's most densely populated areas.

Citizen groups are also resisting the acceptance of such facilities, with a not-in-my-backyard attitude. In addition to the potential hazard to humans in the event of an accident, they fear the locating of plants along their coasts will hurt tourism and raise air pollution risks due to at-sea burning.

According to Jack J. Schramm, director of government affairs at Waste Management Incorporation, residents along the Gulf Coast want a guarantee that an accident will never occur, a request that Schramm calls "impossible" to fulfill.

Risks and benefits must be carefully assessed when dealing with the transportation, storage, and incineration of toxic wastes in the ocean. It seems fair to ask: if a risk/benefit analysis applies, then let it be carried out and a just conclusion announced, if such a conclusion can be found.

OTHER OCEAN DUMPING
PROBLEMS

While at-sea disposal of hazardous industrial materials is a major concern, other waste problems exist. For years the ocean has been used as a catchall for nontoxic industrial wastes, nuclear wastes, sewage sludge, dredged material, and much more. And, in many parts of the world, it still is.

One of the most controversial topics regarding ocean dumping in recent years has been that of dumping sewage sludge, in particular in the New York Bight dump site. In 1981 the EPA took the City of New York to court in an attempt to stop the operation of this site, used for the disposal of over 7 million tons of contaminated sludge each year. The court upheld the City of New York's plea to continue dumping, despite the fact that this dumping was damaging the coastal environment and in conflict with provisions against dumping in both national and international law.

Many former ocean-dumping cities had been compelled to implement land-based sludge-management programs. Indeed, 96 percent of all sewage sludge generated in the United States is now disposed of by means other than ocean dumping. Why then, asked the EPA and National Wildlife Federation, can't New York and New Jersey use the other means?

The EPA presented a number of facts about the damage caused to the ocean environment and marine life around the site. The states of New York and New Jersey argued that their dumping was not the cause of much of the damage. Both sides spent millions of dollars in research

*Garbage barge being pushed to sea
off the coast of New York City.*

and documentation. Most of this documentation produced by each side was contradicted by documention produced by the other.

The EPA, for example, said that dumping had caused vast decreases in fish populations and the contamination of shellfish in the area. New York City, on the other hand, tried to show that the few instances of increased contaminant levels in area fish and shellfish were more likely caused by sources other than sludge dumping.

Another point brought up was that the dump zone was situated in a region of heavy commercial and recreational navigation; locating ocean dump zones in such regions is forbidden by national law. The City revealed that the Coast Guard had concluded that sludge-dumping activities were not a navigation hazard and that the use of the site could actually increase twofold with proper scheduling. Additional conflicts regarding the site included effects on beaches, shorelines, and commercial fishing among others.

As an alternative to the Bight site, the EPA offered the so-called "106-mile" (171-km) site, so called because of its distance from the coastline. After much discussion, it appears that this will in fact become the new dump site for New York and New Jersey sewage sludge. According to the EPA's Jack E. Ravin, dumping activities are gradually closing at the old site and moving to the new location. Though this is not an all-out success, the EPA feels it has won an initial battle. At the same time, New York and New Jersey feel they have saved money by not having to locate and construct land-based disposal areas.

DREDGE DUMPING

Ninety percent of all current ocean dumping in the United States consists of dredged material and is carried out by the U.S. Army Corps of Engineers (ACOE). The ACOE is responsible for maintaining over 25,000 miles (40,000 km) of navigable waterways and improved channels, over 155 commercial harbors and ports, and more than 400 small boat harbors. This is a large task, often calling for dredging.

Dredging generates tons of waste material—often contaminated to varying degrees by toxic pollutants. Recent studies in the New York harbor region revealed a number of such pollutants in dredged compounds. Similarly, an analysis of dredged matter from the Hudson River identified hundreds of waste chemicals that stemmed from 254 industrial and municipal sources. This is the type of material dumped at one of 131 ocean sites designated for such activity by the EPA. Only a handful of these sites have actually been studied, and many have not been used in recent years.

Consequently, the dumping of contaminated dredged material into the ocean merely transfers the pollutants to the new area, hindering local marine life in the process.

Not all dredged material is contaminated, and many experts believe that chemical composition alone is not a true or reliable indicator of contaminants in dredged materials. Heavy metals are a good example. All natural sediments contain them to varying degrees. Therefore, chemical analysis may overstate the potential toxicity of dredged samples.

The U.S. Congress imposed phaseout periods in the early 1980s for the ocean dumping of harmful wastes, such as toxic materials and sewage sludge. No such deadline exists or has been proposed for dredged material. In addition, no convincing evidence exists of a risk factor to health or the environment, perhaps because scientific tests for such risks are still under development. Regulatory standards are very limited.

Some people take all this as an indication that the methods used are safe. Environmentalists regard dredge dumping as a potential risk to combat now before it becomes a major problem. And those who hold the power to institute regulations tend to sway politically from one extreme to the other.

SELECTED READING

Aitken, Donald. "The Marine Environment: A Global Prospective." *Sierra Club Bulletin*, June 1971.

Barton, Robert. *The Oceans*. New York: Facts on File, 1980.

Boxer, Barbara. "Key Observers Comment on Ocean Pollution." *EPA Journal*, November 1984.

Brown, Lester R. "Fish Farming." The Futurist, October 1985.

Carson, Rachel. *The Sea Around Us*. New York: Oxford University Press, 1961.

Clarke, Samuel H. "Highlights in Marine Research." U.S. Geological Survey, 1984.

Colwell, Rita R. "Biotechnology in the Marine Sciences." *Science*, 7 October, 1983.

Colwell, Rita R. "The Industrial Potential of Marine Biotechnology." *Oceanus*, Spring 1984.

Colwell, R., Pariser, E., and Sinskey, A. (eds.). *Biotechnology in the Marine Sciences*. New York: Wiley, 1984.

Conservation Foundation. "Can We Count on Fisheries to Fight Hunger?" *Conservation Foundation Letter* March–April 1985.

Conservation Foundation. "Dig We Must: Nations Eye Deepsea Minerals." *Conservation Foundation Letter,* April 1981.

Cook, David. *Ocean Life.* New York: Crown, 1985.

Cousteau, Jacques Yves. "The Ocean." *National Geographic,* December 1981.

Dubach, Howard W., and Taber, Robert W. *1001 Questions Answered About the Oceans and Oceanography.* New York: Dodd, Mead & Co., 1972.

Ellers, Fred S. "Advanced Offshore Oil Platforms." *Scientific American,* April 1982.

Food and Agriculture Organization of the United Nations. "Yearbook of Fishery Statistics 1983." Vols. 56, 57. FAO, 1984.

Gorman, Brian. "OTEC: The Sleeping Giant." U.S. National Oceanic and Atmospheric Administration, Fall 1981.

Henrickson, Robert. *The Ocean Almanac.* Garden City, N.Y.: Doubleday, 1984.

Idyll, C. P .(ed.) *Exploring the Ocean World.* New York: Crowell, 1972.

Kamlet, Kenneth S. "Key Observers Comment on Ocean Pollution." *EPA Journal,* November 1984.

Ketchum, B., Kester, D., Park, P. (eds.). *Ocean Dumping of Industrial Wastes.* New York: Plenum, 1981.

Lawless, James. "OTEC: A Promising New Source of Energy." U.S. National Oceanic and Atmospheric Administration, Fall 1981.

Lovell, R. T. "Fish Farming is Here to Stay." *Science of Food and Agriculture,* Summer 1985.

McGregor, Bonnie A., and Lockwood, Millington. *Mapping and Research in the Exclusive Economic Zone.* Washington, D.C.: U.S. Geological Survey and U.S. National Oceanic and Atmospheric Administration, n.d.

Parker, Henry S. *Exploring the Oceans.* Englewood Cliffs, N.J.: Prentice-Hall, 1985.

Perry, J. H. *Romance of the Sea*. Washington, D.C.: The National Geographic Society, 1981.

Ravan, Jack E. "The Job of Protecting the Seas." *EPA Journal*, November 1984.

Richardson, Jacques G. "Managing the Ocean." Mt. Airy, Md.: Lomond Publications, 1985.

Simon, Anne W. *Neptune's Revenge*. New York: Watts, 1984.

I N D E X

*Italicized page numbers
refer to illustrations.*

Abalone, 37
Adey, Walter H., 71–72
Algae. *See* Seaweed
Alvin (submersible vehicle),
    95, *96*
Anemones, 35
Animal feed, 44, 72
Apollo One (incinerator
    ship), 113, *114, 115*
Aquaculture, 15, 54–55
    advantages of, 58–60
    biotechnology and, 37
    capturing and rearing
        young, 62–63, *64,*
        65–66
    egg-incubation-
        hatching system, 60,
        61, 62

history of, 29
modern techniques, 71
problems in, 74–76
protein energy of
    farmed fish, 55, 58
rearing and releasing,
    66, *67,* 68, *69,* 70–
    71
of seaweed, 71–72, *73,*
    74

Barnacles, 40, 50–51
Biodegrading, 38
Biotechnology, 34–36
    and aquaculture, 37
    and biodegrading, 38
    business concerns, 40–
        41
    and fouling, 38–40
    and industrial
        chemicals, 36

Boxer, Barbara, 92
Bromine, 32, 78–79

Cameos, 27–28
Catch limits, 52
Construction materials,
    79–80
Coral, 35, 38–39
Coring, 94–95
Cousteau, Jacques-Yves, 14

Dadswell, Michael, 102
Desalinization, 92, 94, 107

Elements, 78–79
Energy sources, 16, 99
    thermal energy, 102–4,
    105, 106–7
    tidal energy, 100–2
    wave power, 99–100
Exclusive Economic Zones
    (EEZ), 48, *49,* 50, 80,
    89

Fish and shellfish
    nutrients in, 42, 44
    preservation methods,
    46, *47,* 48
    protein energy, 55, 58
    unconventional species,
    utilization of, 50–52
Fishing, commercial, 15, 42,
    43, 44, *56, 57*
    dwindling food sources
    and, 50–53, 54
    fishing grounds, 48, *49,*
    50

history of, 20, *21,* 22,
    23, 24
    influences in, 45–48
    leading countries, *45*
Fishing, sport, 71
Fouling, 38–40
Freshwater conversion, 92,
    94
Fry, 66, *70*

Geology, marine, 94–95, *96,*
    97–98
Glaude, Georges, 102–3
GLORIA (sonar system),
    96, 97, 97
Gosling, Burton B., 84
Gypsum, 32

Hillman, C. Thomas, 84
History of ocean commer-
    cialization, 19–20
    commercial fishing, 20,
    21, 22, *23,* 24
    jewelry, 27–28
    marine mammal
    business, 24, *25, 26,*
    27
    marine products, 29,
    30, 31
    modern techniques,
    31–33
Hydrocarbons, 88–89
Hydrothermal ore de-
    posits, *82,* 83

Incineration, 110–13

Incineration (*continued*)
Apollo One, operation
of, 113, *114,* 115
locations for, 115–16
marine transfer ter-
minals, 116–18
Industrial chemicals, 36
Iodine, 32, 78

Jewelry, 27–28

Kamlet, Kenneth S., 109
Krill, 51–52

Lawless, James, 103
Lobster farming, 71
Lovell, R. T., 58

Magnesium, 32, 78, 79
Mammals, marine, 24, *25,*
26, 27
Medicines, 35, 40
Methane production, 72
Mineral resources, 16–17,
31–32, 79
construction materials,
79–80
hydrocarbons, 88–89
hydrothermal ore
deposits, *82,* 83
manganese nodules,
83–84, *85*
phosphorites, 80–81
placer deposits, 81, 83
Monkfish, *51*
Morse, D. E., 37

Natural gas, 16, 33
Nodules, 83–84, *85*
mining of, 17, 31, *86,*
87–88

Ocean exploration, history
of, 19–20
Oceanography, 31
Oil drilling, 16, 32–33, 77,
88–89, *90,* 95, 97
Oil spills, 91
Outer Continental Shelf
(OCS) leasing, 89, 91–92
Oyster farming, 60, *61,* 62

Pearls, 28
Phosphorites, 80–81
Placer deposits, 81, 83
Pollution, 14, 17
and aquaculture, 74
biodegrading and, 38
dredge dumping and,
121
ocean incineration and,
110–13, 115
salmon ranching and,
71
sludge dumping and,
118, 120
Polyculture, 65
Potash, 32

Ravin, Jack E., 115, 120
Reagan, Ronald, 48
Red tide, 74
Resources, marine, 77. *See
also specific resources*

Rittschof, Dan, 39
Roosevelt, Christopher, 14–15

Salmon ranching, 15, 66, 68, 70–71
Salt production, 31–32, *93*
Sand mining, 80
Schramm, Jack J., 117
Sea ranching, 15
Seal hunting, 24, 24, 27
Seaweed, 29, 78, 81
    cultivation of, 71–72, *73, 74*
Seismic surveys, 95, 97
Sewage sludge, 118, 120
Shad fishing, 102
Shrimp farming, 71
Side-scan sonar, 97
Smolt, 68

Soda, 32
Sponges, 29, *30,* 31, 35, 36
Submersible vehicles, 95, *96*

Thermal energy, 102–4, *105,* 106–7
Thomson, C. Wyville, 32
Tidal hydroelectric dams, 16, 99, 100–2
Tuna farming, 63
Turtle farming, 63, *64,* 65

Waste disposal, 17, 108–10
    dredge dumping, 120–21
    problems in, 118, *119,* 120.
    See also Incineration
Welling, Conrad G., 84, 87
Whaling, 24, *25, 26,* 52